R-3420

Castro, Cuba, and the World

Edward Gonzalez, David Ronfeldt

June 1986

Rand
1700 MAIN STREET
P.O. BOX 2138
SANTA MONICA, CA 90406-2138

PREFACE

This report provides a new profile of Fidel Castro's mindset and world view. It combines an analysis of the Cuban leader's ambitions and patterns of behavior as a political actor with assessments of Cuba's current domestic and international situations, in order to analyze his foreign policy options through the late 1980s.

Castro is at a crucial juncture at home and abroad. The leadership changes that he made before and at the Third Congress of the Communist Party of Cuba in February 1986, his recent return to a radical economic posture at home, and his shrill attacks on the United States over its military actions against Libya all testify once again to the volatility—and continued centrality—of his personal rule. In addition, his setback in Grenada and other difficulties suggest that he has been frustrated by his lack of compensating triumphs on the international front. Thus his foreign policy remains in flux and new questions arise as to whether his future international behavior will ultimately settle on a more moderate or a newly aggressive course. Accordingly, this study should be of interest to specialists and policy analysts concerned with Cuba, as well as to other members of the broader U.S. policy community.

SUMMARY

After 27 years in power, has Fidel Castro become a mellower revolutionary, no longer the rebellious radical of the past? Now approaching 60 years of age, he has displayed signs of moderation: He signed a migration agreement with the United States in December 1984, conversed with visiting U.S. bishops the following January, and gave a series of extensive interviews to U.S. and foreign media. He has, however, also shown flashes of his earlier self, as in his angry suspension of the migration agreement when Radio Martí started broadcasting in May 1985. Still, it was an older Fidel who recently discoursed extensively on religion and commenced a "dialogue" with the Catholic Church at home and abroad.

Has Castro in fact become less revolutionary, less confrontational, and less militantly anti-U.S.? Has he become more reasonable and pragmatic as a result of domestic economic problems, Soviet pressures, and new international realities? Is a "new Fidel" emerging?

This study concludes that the answer to all these questions is "No." Castro continues to exhibit the same ambitions and behavioral patterns that have characterized his rule for more than a quarter of a century. The reasons for such constancy lie in his extraordinary mindset and a mode of behavior that has served him well since childhood.

Castro's mindset and behavior reflect many traditional tendencies in Latin American political culture, for example, *caudillismo* and nationalism. Yet he carries these tendencies to such an extreme and he remains such an extraordinary phenomenon that we have developed new concepts for analyzing his mindset and his *modus operandi* against adversaries.

CASTRO'S MINDSET: A HUBRIS-NEMESIS COMPLEX

To analyze Castro as a political actor, this study begins by turning to two concepts from Greek mythology, hubris and nemesis. These concepts illuminate the core of Castro's mindset, and in combination they enable the identification of a "hubris-nemesis complex" that reflects two of Castro's most basic drives: his unrelenting ambition for power and his continuing animosity toward the United States.

The Traditional Dynamic: Hubris Versus Nemesis

Hubris is the capital sin of personal pride, a pretension to act like a god while failing to observe the established balance of man and nature. Hubris inflates a person to exceed the fate and fortune ordained by the gods, thereby arousing their envy and anger.

Nemesis was the obscure goddess of divine retribution, righteous anger, and Olympian vengeance. She intervened in human affairs to restore equilibrium when it had been disturbed, usually by persons who had attained excessive power and wealth. Hubris in particular attracted Nemesis, who then humiliated and destroyed those who manifested it, often by means of terror and devastation.

A New Dynamic: Hubris and Nemesis Fused

As a powerful charismatic leader, Castro has often shown himself to be filled with hubris. He arrogates to himself virtually all power in Cuba, pursues grandiose ambitions as a global actor, and seeks immortality as the force that will bring down a far more powerful adversary. He may thus seem ripe for doing something that will lead to his downfall.

Yet looking at Castro this way ignores the fact that in addition to his hubris, he has also internalized a self-appointed role as the nemesis of the world's greatest power, the United States. As long ago as 1958, he confided to a close revolutionary supporter:

> When I saw rockets firing . . . I swore to myself that the North Americans were going to pay dearly for what they were doing. When this war is over a much wider and bigger war will commence for me: the war I am going to wage against them. I am aware that this is my true destiny.[1]

Accordingly, Castro's hubris is no ordinary hubris, for a crucial part of it is to play the role of nemesis. The two forces appear to have coalesced to impart incredible energy, ambition, and dynamism. To be as powerful as his hubris requires, he must fulfill a role as the nemesis of the United States, and this in turn requires him to possess absolute power at home and relentlessly seek to expand it abroad.

The "hubris-nemesis complex" helps to illuminate why Castro constantly exhibits certain distinctive traits:

---

[1]From Rolando E. Bonachea and Nelson P. Valdés (eds.), *Revolutionary Struggle, 1947-1958: Volume 1 of the Selected Works of Fidel Castro*, Cambridge, Mass.: The MIT Press, 1972, p. 379.

- *A constructive-destructive messianism.* Castro sees himself fulfilling, if not exceeding, the historical legacies of Simón Bolívar and José Martí. He sets goals that are often unattainable or unreasonable, as exemplified by his order to Cuban contingents on Grenada not to surrender to U.S. forces.
- *High ideals that moralize violence.* Castro's overall vision and high-minded rhetoric ultimately require wreaking a great deal of destructive violence abroad.
- *A sense of struggle that may become self-sacrificial.* Castro relishes overcoming terrible odds, thereby confirming his sense of invincibility. He thrives on defying the United States. Though not suicidal, he might prefer martyrdom to surrender or humiliation.
- *Absolute power, demanding unquestioning loyalty and attention.* Castro cannot tolerate being opposed, ignored, abandoned, or upstaged, whether at home or abroad. He pursues an ambitious "internationalist" foreign policy that includes sending combat troops overseas and actively assisting guerrilla movements.

Thus it would be an error to view Castro as just another quixotic but essentially pragmatic actor who will make ordinary cost-benefit calculations of his and Cuba's interests. His mindset is geared to resisting rather than responding to U.S. economic inducements and military threats; it does not permit any compromise or accommodation with the United States on core issues. It was this mindset that impelled him toward military adventurism in Angola and Ethiopia precisely at a time when the Ford and especially the Carter administrations were actively seeking more normalized relations with Cuba. Although he remains ready to put Cuba at risk, Castro can feign moderation to preserve his power while he waits to advance his grand long-term ambitions.

CASTRO'S *MODUS OPERANDI* AGAINST ADVERSARIES

Castro has developed a unique *modus operandi* for dealing with his adversaries, and sometimes his allies. The recurrent behavioral traits that make up this pattern have exhibited remarkable constancy from Castro's childhood through the present day.

Castro as a Child and Youth: El Niño Malcriado

As the *niño malcriado,* or misbehaving child, and later as a student politician and revolutionary leader, Castro developed a pattern of conflictive, duplicitous behavior that enabled him to get his way with parents, guardians, schoolteachers, and fellow students, and subsequently to gain power and assert himself on the world stage:

- *Violence-prone rebelliousness, which, even when risky, often yielded much higher returns than conformity*—evidenced by his repeated fistfights to gain supremacy over his schoolmates, his revolutionary career against Batista, and his later efforts to promote revolution elsewhere.
- *Manipulative confrontation to force concessions from allies as well as adversaries*—first manifested when he defied his guardians when he was seven years old in order to be sent to boarding school, this trait has also characterized his dealings with both the Soviets and the United States.
- *Extortion to deter or intimidate an opponent*—as when he threatened to set fire to his parents' home unless he was allowed to return to school, and currently when he manipulates revolutionary subversion against Latin American governments that oppose him and align themselves with the United States.
- *Vengeful punishment against those who have thwarted him*—he threatened to shoot a schoolmate who had beaten him up, and he has likewise threatened his internal enemies and those who have opposed him on the international front, including the Venezuelan government in the 1960s and the Colombian government after 1979.
- *Claiming high principles to mask his own self-interest*—he justified his rebellious childhood behavior on the basis of unfair parental authority, and he now actively supports violent movements on the basis of righting social injustices, extending revolutionary solidarity, and engaging in self-defense.
- *Deceitfulness to conceal his intentions*—he falsified his grades and forged his parents' signatures in grade school, disguised his Marxism-Leninism upon coming to power, and presently masks his involvements in Central America and Cuba's domestic problems and human rights abuses.

Later Revolutionary Traits: The *Fidelista* Mentality

Castro's experiences during the revolutionary struggle of the 1950s solidified a *fidelista* mentality that, beginning with the attack on the Moncada barracks in 1953, has included a penchant for:

- *Revolutionary maximalism, in which he seeks major strategic breakthroughs*—as exemplified by his initial realignment with

the Soviets in 1959–60, his 1970 sugar harvest goal of 10 million tons, and his plunge into Africa a decade ago.
- *High risk-taking in ventures that he believes can potentially yield high payoffs*—as evidenced most recently by his involvements in Grenada, Nicaragua, and El Salvador.

The guerrilla struggle in the Sierra Maestra strengthened Castro's radical propensities but added these prudential components:

- *Primacy of subjective forces, whereby he remains convinced that human volition can overcome structural constraints*—as evidenced by the Rebel Army's victory over Batista, Cuba's ascendancy in world politics, and Castro's success in coping with the "Colossus of the North."
- *Strategic opportunism in the belief that historical shifts and openings must be seized*—e.g., Cuba's exploitation of developments in Africa and Central America, and the Soviet Union's expansionist surge of the 1970s.
- *Tactical pragmatism to avoid a head-on collision or strategic loss*—as occurred when he maneuvered to limit Cuba's intervention in the Grenadian crisis to the Cuban forces on the island.

Constancy in Strategic Goals Despite Tactical Shifts

Castro has continually held onto a set of "maximalist" objectives that have imparted an offensive quality to his international behavior. These objectives include leading the Third World struggle against U.S. imperialism, extending Cuba's global influence and presence, promoting the rise of new revolutionary-left regimes in Africa and Latin America, increasing Cuba's military capabilities, and gaining a wider latitude of action through leverage over Moscow.

These power-maximizing goals cannot be realized through pragmatic or prudent behavior. Yet at times Castro does resort to such behavior. Thus, his *modus operandi* fits the following syllogism:

- Under certain conditions, pragmatism may be required to buy time, conserve power, and protect realized gains.
- Rebelliousness, radicalism, and strategic opportunism, however, are the only means by which long-term maximum objectives can be attained.
- Pragmatism is thus a short-term tactic that must not stand in the way of resuming the revolutionary offensive when the opportunity reemerges.

Castro is currently constrained from pursuing his maximum goals. Whether he resumes the offensive soon will depend in large part on his reading of Cuba's internal situation and the international correlation of forces.

CASTRO AND CUBA

On the domestic scene, Castro's personal power remains secure and his regime rests on a powerful state apparatus for assuring defense, security, and social control. Still, he faces new political and economic challenges, as well as Soviet pressures for change, that are taxing his leadership abilities. These problems were reflected in the Third Congress of the Communist Party of Cuba (PCC), held in February 1986.

Managing and Reconstituting Elite Coalitions

Castro cannot rule alone. Within the top echelons of Cuba's elite, he must maintain a balance among the older generation of guerrilla veterans and loyalists and the younger generation of civilian and military elites whose expertise is needed to run the government and implement Cuba's "internationalist" missions. Thus he has had to make room for the "children of the revolution" in the new Central Committee of the PCC. Because of domestic and foreign criticisms, he has also had to address the issue of racial discrimination. While the number of Afro-Cubans in the PCC Political Bureau remains unchanged, Castro appears to have increased the percentage of blacks and mulattoes among the regular and alternate members of the new Central Committee, even though Cuba's large Afro-Cuban population is still underrepresented.

In the Political Bureau, Castro was obliged to retire three *fidelista* guerrilla veterans (the so-called *historicos*)—including the former Minister of Interior, Ramiro Valdés—because of their incompetence. At the same time, the elevation of two prominent *raúlistas* to full membership in the ruling Party organ strengthened the position of Fidel's brother Raúl, who was formally confirmed as Fidel's designated successor.

The reshuffling of high government and Party officials that started in early 1985 and continued through the Third Party Congress stems partly from Soviet pressures for administrative reforms, the appointment of more competent leaders, and more efficient management of the economy. Castro may have defused these pressures by appointing *raúlistas*, who are generally presumed to be more competent and more pro-Soviet than the *fidelistas*. Yet this also means the Castro dynasty has become even more entrenched. Fidel remains very much in command because he can count on the loyalty of his brother, and the *fidelistas* and *raúlistas* now dominate the Political Bureau to a greater extent than before.[2]

Controlling the Military and Society

Castro cannot ignore the Revolutionary Armed Forces (FAR) because of their institutional strength and links to the Soviet military. There are signs that the younger, battle-tested, more professional officer class within the FAR is becoming restless over Castro's doctrine of "people's war," promotional issues, and Cuba's overseas military commitments, particularly in Angola. Castro may have elevated Division General Abelardo Colomé, a First Vice Minister in the Ministry of the FAR, to full membership in the Political Bureau to assuage the military's institutional interests or to further assure the Party's control over the FAR.

Perhaps to counterbalance the FAR, Castro has continued the buildup of the Territorial Troop Militia (MTT), which now has 1.5 million members. Unlike the FAR, the MTT is unencumbered by institutional or professional links to the Soviet military and is led directly by the PCC. Providing the mass base for the new "people's war" doctrine, the MTT can be used not only to defend the island in the event of U.S. aggression, but also (and perhaps more likely) to release FAR units for future military missions abroad. Meanwhile, the MTT has enabled Castro to militarize society in order to heighten social control and revive the revolutionary commitment of the popular masses.

New Economic Priorities

Pressed by Moscow, Castro launched the new "economic war of the whole people" at the end of 1984. Highest priority was to be given to making efficient use of Soviet economic assistance, increasing production, and fulfilling trade obligations. But drought, Hurricane Kate, and collapsing oil prices promise lower foreign exchange earnings on the international market for Cuban sugar exports and (Soviet-supplied) petroleum reexports. Even if sugar prices continue to rise, Cuba might not be able to expand its sugar exports to the West because of its trade commitments to the Soviet bloc. And despite its 1982 investment law,

---

[2]The 14-member Bureau includes six *fidelistas* and five *raúlistas*.

the Castro regime has thus far been unable to attract wary Western investors to Cuba.

At the Third Party Congress, Castro read a litany of ills that plague Cuba's mismanaged and malfunctioning economy. But he is fundamentally opposed to decentralization and other liberalizing reforms—witness his abolition in May 1986 of the six-year-old experiment with free peasant markets on the grounds that it was giving rise to neocapitalism. Unless the Soviet Union itself adopts Hungarian-type reforms, which appears unlikely, there is little prospect of the new generation of technocrats doing so on their own in Cuba.

Implications: The Need to Buy Time and Triumph Anew

The current domestic situation cannot be to Castro's liking: He can no longer expect dramatic achievements, and he will be frustrated by seemingly intractable economic problems. He sees that Cuba's internal situation is increasingly a matter of administration rather than leadership. Castro is thus likely to turn the day-to-day administration of the government and economy over to Raúl. This arrangement would enable Fidel to preserve his power, including ultimate veto power over major policy decisions, and to meet Soviet demands for more efficient administration. It would also allow him to concentrate on international matters, the area where he might be best able to triumph anew.

CASTRO AND THE WORLD

Castro faces an international environment that is virtually the reverse of what it was a decade ago. Shifts in "the international correlation of forces" have created uncertainties as to which superpower is stronger and which will ultimately win. This constrains Castro's maximalist ambitions.

Superpower Constraints

The United States. Castro is concerned over the resurgence of U.S. military might, political resolve, and public policy consensus. He has had great difficulty in trying to manipulate the current U.S. administration and political process to Cuba's advantage. Lacking security guarantees from Moscow, he knows that Cuba remains the most exposed salient in the Soviet Union's empire. In the event of an East-West or even a U.S.-Nicaraguan crisis, Cuba could become a U.S. target because of its potential threat to critical U.S. sea lanes of communication in the Caribbean. In violently condemning the recent U.S. military action against the Khaddafi regime, he has indicated that he is disturbed over its implications.

The Soviet Union. Castro sees that the Gorbachev regime is shifting priorities to domestic economic issues and demanding better economic performance from its clients, including Cuba. Gorbachev appears intent on stabilizing superpower relations and less inclined to launch a new expansionist drive into the Third World—although his regime will surely work to consolidate its gains in Afghanistan, Angola, and Nicaragua. Gorbachev's keynote address at the Twenty-Seventh CPSU Party Congress in February 1986 contained none of the traditional Kremlin pledges to support "wars of national liberation," the first such omission at a Party Congress in thirty years. Castro must find this apparent Soviet deemphasis on the Third World disquieting, because this is where he has been able to fulfill his maximalist ambitions, particularly when he has had Soviet backing. Overall, he faces a tougher and less familiar Soviet leadership under Gorbachev that could shift the foundations of the Soviet-Cuban relationship from ideological, political, and strategic underpinnings to new administrative and economic priorities—hardly Castro's strengths.

The Third World: Risks, Schisms, and Few Opportunities

While Castro is intent upon consolidating revolutionary advances in Angola and Nicaragua, current trends in the Third World and the North-South struggle are surely not to his liking:

- Potential opportunities loom in southern Africa, but Cuba may be tied down in a costly war in Angola.
- Prospects for revolutions are receding in Central America, while the defense of Nicaragua may jeopardize Cuba's own security.
- The U.S.-led intervention in Grenada and the recent ouster of the Duvalier regime from Haiti have strengthened U.S. influence in the Caribbean.
- Opportunities for exploiting the Latin American debt crisis are offset by the renewal of the region's democratic tendencies and overriding interests in good economic relations with the West.
- The Non-Aligned Movement and the militant campaign for a "new international economic order" have declined in importance as anti-U.S. and anti-imperialist vehicles.
- The newly industrializing capitalist-oriented countries of Southeast Asia provide successful performance models that stand in contrast to Cuba and other struggling socialist economies.

- Other militantly anti-American countries, notably Libya and Iran, have gained worldwide attention in recent years, but far from being willing allies of Cuba, they have acted more as competitors.

While Castro may have opportunities in southern Africa and parts of the Caribbean Basin, taking advantage of them will entail far higher risks than was the case in the middle to late 1970s. If aggressive military adventurism is ruled out, however, he may still attempt revolutionary extortion against governments that stand in the way of his ambitions (e.g., Honduras).

Implications: Be Prudent While Awaiting New Opportunities

These generally adverse developments have obliged Castro to alter course momentarily and pursue a more prudent posture. Thus, he presented himself as Latin America's champion on the debt issue during 1985, and he cultivated U.S. Catholic bishops and radical priests from around the world, presenting his views in a new book about liberation theology. He may be aiming to split the Catholic Church and create a new united front among radical Catholics and Marxists that would help shield Nicaragua and Cuba from U.S. aggression.

Castro's moves on these fronts, however, are not leading to the kinds of breakthroughs that could revitalize his leadership image and gratify his maximalist ambitions. Overall, this could be quite frustrating to him, especially as his youth ebbs away.

CASTRO'S FUTURE OPTIONS

Castro's basic patterns of thinking and acting are not likely to change. As he maneuvers through the rest of the Reagan administration's term of office, he will almost certainly opt for one of the two types of international strategies that have characterized his behavior in the past, *tactical pragmatism* or *revolutionary maximalism*.

International Strategies

The continuation of *a defensive policy of tactical pragmatism* would assure the security of Castro's regime and preserve established gains. This minimalist posture, using political initiatives to disarm or confuse adversaries, would reflect not only his concern for his nation's security, but also a lack of opportunity to do anything truly ambitious. Such a posture would not mean accommodation with the United States or changes in Cuba's commitments to the Soviet Union, Nicaragua, and Angola, nor would it imply abandonment of revolutionary subversion. This prudent stance must be understood, rather, as relative to Castro's maximalist posture.

Alternatively, Castro could once again turn to *an offensive policy of revolutionary maximalism*, with the goals of leading the Third World struggle against the United States, extending Cuba's influence in Africa and Latin America, promoting the rise of Marxist regimes in the Caribbean Basin, extending Cuba's capabilities as a regional and global actor, and regaining leverage vis-à-vis the Soviet Union. This would involve the employment of both conventional (military) and unconventional (guerrilla) forms of violence. Violence is an essential element of Castro's *modus operandi*; it has led to his greatest triumphs at home and abroad.

Alternative Scenarios

The strategic option Castro chooses for the rest of the 1980s will depend on his assessment of (1) Cuba's domestic situation, (2) the U.S. foreign policy posture, (3) the Soviet foreign policy posture, (4) the openings in the Third World, and (5) the situation facing Cuba's clients. Of these five variables, the Soviet Union's international posture is most critical to Castro because, ultimately, Soviet policies set the basic parameters for his behavior. The following illustrative scenarios suggest how these factors may play out in Castro's future assessment of his policy options.

Tactical Pragmatism. If all five factors remain essentially as they are today, Castro will find that his possibilities for revolutionary maximalism are limited. His domestic situation would not necessarily constrain his actions abroad, but the international arena would: There would be major risks (U.S. power and resolve to roll back Communism) and constraints (a Soviet emphasis on consolidating rather than expanding present gains), and few opportunities for new breakthroughs (the Third World arena). Hence, as he has done since the Grenada debacle of 1983, Castro would continue to opt for a stratagem of tactical pragmatism.

Nicaragua and Angola might still present limited opportunities for Cuba, partly because the Soviets want to consolidate the Marxist-Leninist regimes there. If so, then Cuban advisers might continue working with the Sandinista army, while Cuban military personnel might support the MPLA (Popular Movement for the Liberation of Angola) forces in their offensive against UNITA (the National Union for the Total Independence of Angola). In both situations, Castro would limit the level of direct Cuban involvement in combat operations, thereby minimizing his military and political risks.

Meanwhile, Havana's policy of solidarity with and training of Latin American revolutionaries would be maintained. Because of the absence of major targets of opportunity, however, Castro would be careful about revolutionary subversion. He would move on the diplomatic, political, and religious fronts to attract favorable publicity and defuse reaction to his policies.

Revolutionary Maximalism. If the domestic and U.S. factors remained the same, but the Soviet, Third World, and client-regime factors became more favorable, Castro would be more inclined to resume a revolutionary maximalist course, despite the risks involved. Such a situation could arise if the Soviets became bolder in the Third World, the South African situation deteriorated, and Nicaragua and Angola began winning their respective wars against the Contras and UNITA.

In this scenario, however, the prospect of direct U.S. intervention to oust the Sandinistas might also increase. A prospective U.S. intervention in Nicaragua would pose a serious dilemma: Castro would risk losing an important ally if he did not defend Nicaragua, but he might risk a military showdown with the United States if he tried to assist Managua directly, either unilaterally or multilaterally through Cuban and Latin American "volunteers."

To escape such a dilemma, Castro might prefer to regain the revolutionary offensive in southern Africa, perhaps even trying to link a Cuban escalation in Angola with Nicaragua's security. With Soviet support, Cuban forces could assume a direct and enlarged combat role in Angola. That role could be expanded into Namibia and perhaps even into troubled South Africa by actively backing SWAPO (the South-West African People's Organization) and the ANC (African National Congress), respectively. Castro could justify such a policy as a national war of liberation against South Africa's apartheid regime, thereby rallying Black Africa's support and legitimizing the Soviet foothold in southern Africa.

Such a gambit would be tantamount to a *fidelista* version of lateral escalation, whereby Castro would seek to intensify crisis conditions in southern Africa in order to distract and constrain the United States from intervening in Nicaragua. Were he to succeed in this instance, he would triumph anew on both the African and Central American fronts.

He would, of course, have to face many practical problems and risks—among them, logistical difficulties in southern Africa, likely clashes with superior South African forces, overextension of Cuba's military commitments, increased vulnerability to U.S. counterescalation in Nicaragua, and likely resistance from the Cuban military. Nevertheless, his capacity to think globally and act as a player on the world stage should not be underestimated as it was in the 1970s. Nor should it be forgotten that his hubris-nemesis complex and audacious *modus operandi* could lead him to try to deal the United States a strategic defeat through renewed Cuban military (or guerrilla) involvement in the Third World, particularly in southern Africa.

CONTENTS

PREFACE iii

SUMMARY v

Section
I. THE IMPORTANCE OF ANALYZING CASTRO 1

II. CASTRO'S MINDSET: A HUBRIS-NEMESIS COMPLEX . 3
   Internal Hubris Versus External Nemesis:
      The Traditional Dynamic 5
   Hubris and Nemesis Combined in the Same Person: ....
      A New Concept 6
   The Case of Castro 13
   Development and Durability of the Complex 30

III. CASTRO'S *MODUS OPERANDI* 33
   The Charismatic *Caudillo* 33
   El Niño Malcriado: Rebelliousness
      and Violence 35
   El Niño Malcriado: The Artful Dissembler 45
   Radicalism, Opportunism, and Tactical Pragmatism:
      The *Fidelista* Mentality 49
   Constancy over Change 58

IV. CASTRO AND CUBA 63
   Attention to Domestic and International Linkages 64
   Fortress Cuba and Its Vulnerabilities 65
   Maintaining Elite Balances and Support 67
   Controlling the Military 74
   Reviving the Revolutionary Commitment of the Masses .. 79
   New Economic Priorities and Urgencies 80
   Orchestrating Leadership Change: Turning to Raúl 87

V. CASTRO AND THE WORLD 90
   Cuba and the International Correlation of Forces 91
   Shifts in the East-West Struggle 92
   The North-South Struggle: Declining Opportunities,
      New Complexities 101
   New Forces Entering Castro's World View 110
   Castro's Leadership Image Problem: The Need to
      Triumph Anew 117

VI. CASTRO'S FOREIGN POLICY OPTIONS 121
   Two Policy Modes 121
   Key Variables in Castro's Future Policy Calculus 123
   Alternative Situation Scenarios and Castro's Options 125

I. THE IMPORTANCE OF ANALYZING CASTRO

To understand Cuban foreign policy, one must first understand Fidel Castro. Even though Cuba has a more institutionalized and complex political order than before, Castro remains the architect of foreign policy, the final arbiter of policy disputes, and the ultimate authority whose backing must be secured by all political subordinates. As he was more than two and half decades ago, he remains Cuba's undisputed Socialist *caudillo* and *líder máximo*.[1]

There are special reasons for analyzing Castro at this particular time. First, even though his behavior has always lent itself to sensational descriptions, no in-depth study of his personal nature has been done that is relevant to policy analysis. New questions need to be addressed concerning the constancy or change in his extraordinary personality and leadership traits. Some analysts have suggested that age, frustration, and other personal burdens may soon take their toll and may even lead to significant alterations in his behavior toward the United States. At the same time, there are good reasons to emphasize continuities in his charisma, his revolutionary idealism and nationalism, his drive for power and attention, his penchant for defiance and confrontation, and his ingrained animus toward the United States.

Second, Cuba's domestic and international situations are at a critical juncture, and Castro's mindset and world view will have a decisive effect on Cuba's responses. Some elements of his world view may be undergoing significant modifications, especially as a result of the U.S. military intervention in Grenada, U.S. air strikes against Libya, and Soviet policy reassessments regarding the Third World. It is thus important to inquire anew whether Castro's policy direction will change and whether it may even exceed the boundaries of his previous behavior patterns. For example, some observers argue that Castro may finally be ready to consider a genuine rapprochement with the United States, while others contend that he could, in desperation, target places involving vital U.S. interests that he has so far treated with caution (e.g., Mexico, Puerto Rico).

---

[1]Castro's dominance is confirmed by a former insider, Manuel Sánchez Pérez, the Cuban Vice-Minister in the State Committee for Material and Technical Supply, who defected in Spain in December 1985. According to Sánchez, "Fidel Castro continues to be the sole leader, the absolute architect of the system, and there is no important decision which has not been decided by him." (Radio interview with Manuel Sánchez Pérez, conducted by Carlos Alberto Montaner, Madrid, December 1985.)

Against this background, and building on earlier Rand work on Cuba,[2] this study takes a new look at Castro's personal nature, his outward views, and the interactions between them. To enhance our understanding of and ability to predict Castro's (and thus Cuba's) future international behavior, the study offers two new constructs:

- A concept for analyzing Castro's mindset, which we term the "hubris-nemesis complex."
- A set of idiosyncratic behavior patterns that have comprised Castro's *modus operandi* for dealing with adversaries, from his childhood as a *niño malcriado* through his adult political career.

These constructs are not designed to plumb Fidel's psyche from a psychoanalytic or psychobiographic standpoint; they are developed only to illuminate specific aspects of his extraordinary mindset and behavior as a political actor nurtured in Cuba and set on playing an international revolutionary role.

However extraordinary Castro is, he does not act in a void. To provide a further basis for assessing and forecasting his behavior, therefore, the analysis also includes Castro's world view. Based on his statements and actions, and related developments inside and outside of Cuba, the analysis pieces together his likely concerns about:

- Cuba's current domestic situation through and beyond the Third Party Congress.
- The international correlation of forces affecting Cuba and the world today.

In light of these analyses of Castro's mindset, behavior, and world view, the study concludes with a discussion of how he may see his future foreign policy options under different possible scenarios.

---

[2]See Edward Gonzalez and David Ronfeldt, *Post-Revolutionary Cuba in a Changing World*, The Rand Corporation, R-1844-ISA, December 1975; David Ronfeldt, *Superclients and Superpowers, Cuba: Soviet Union/Iran: United States*, The Rand Corporation, P-5945, April 1978; and Edward Gonzalez, *A Strategy for Dealing with Cuba in the 1980s*, The Rand Corporation, R-2954-DOS/AF, September 1982.

II. CASTRO'S MINDSET: A HUBRIS-NEMESIS COMPLEX

What makes Fidel Castro tick? As one of the most striking leaders and personalities of our time, a man of great complexity and ability, he has aroused constant curiosity and concern as to what drives his behavior, what he may do next, and how he may respond to changes in his domestic and international circumstances. To mention just a few traits (some of them contradictory) that most observers and analysts agree on, Castro is known to be power-hungry, ambitious, grandiose, authoritarian, charismatic, dogmatic, pragmatic, opportunistic, idealistic, defiant, rebellious, brilliant, persuasive, charming, and fundamentally anti-U.S. In addition, some psychologists, psychiatrists, and psychoanalysts have expressed views that certain diagnostic concepts (e.g., manic-depressiveness, megalomania, narcissism, paranoia) might apply to aspects of his personality and behavior.

Two tentative schools of thought have emerged among Cuba watchers in recent years: Some observers hold that, despite Castro's great abilities, he is quite irrational, ever capable of wild and dangerous behavior. Others argue that he is generally quite pragmatic, at bottom an opportunist who observes rational limits. Within these schools of thought, some analysts emphasize psychiatric and psychoanalytic explanations of his behavior, while others believe that political idealism, ideology, nationalism, and political culture lie behind many of his thoughts and actions.

There is, of course, much truth to all of this. No single school of thought has yet satisfactorily explained Castro's overall mindset, much less predicted his behavior. We are still far from having a comprehensive and fully informed view of Castro. Like other leaders of his stature, complexity, and mystery, he will always be interpreted in varied ways. Better answers are needed about Castro, however, because the assumptions that policymakers make about his nature may significantly affect the priorities and choices among U.S. options for dealing with Cuba.

Against this background, we begin by offering a new look at Castro's political mindset. We attempt to synthesize what is known about him by turning to two ancient concepts from Greek mythology, hubris and nemesis, which appear to illuminate core aspects of his political nature.

In combination, they define a new concept, the "hubris-nemesis complex,"[1] which

- Reflects two of Castro's basic behavior patterns, his unrelenting ambition for power and his repeated animosity against the United States.
- Reveals how his diverse traits, some of which compete and conflict with others, have combined in a coherent and even logical way.
- May assist in forecasting Castro's behavior, including his responses to U.S. policy.

Although this concept is developed here specifically in relation to Castro, it may also be applicable to other leaders to whom he is sometimes compared.

Because the concept of the "hubris-nemesis complex" is in an early state of formulation and development, the following discussion is exploratory. The concept is not derived from existing psychological, psychiatric, or psychoanalytic constructs, nor is it offered as such. Although it could be linked to such constructs,[2] it can also be linked to anthropological, sociological, and epistemological approaches to analyzing how people look at the world in patterned ways.[3] In other words,

---

[1] The hubris-nemesis complex was first defined in David Ronfeldt, *The Modern Mexican Military: Implications for Mexico's Stability and Security*, The Rand Corporation, N-2288-FF/RC, February 1985, pp. 42–44.

[2] Such constructs include those of the authoritarian personality, the charismatic personality, the messianic personality, the narcissistic personality, and possibly the Icarian personality. In particular, there may be an overlap with concepts of the narcissistic and the Icarian personalities, for both derive from the psychoanalytic implications of basic myths in which different forms of hubris lead to self-destruction. The hubris-nemesis concept introduced here is substantially different because it incorporates the nemesis dimension as an essential part of the personality or mindset. References include T. W. Adorno et al., *The Authoritarian Personality*, New York: Harper Bros., 1950; Ann Ruth Willner, *The Spellbinders: Charismatic Political Leadership*, New Haven: Yale University Press, 1984; Jerrold M. Post, "Dreams of Glory and the Life Cycle: Reflections on the Life Course of Narcissistic Leaders," *Journal of Political and Military Sociology*, Spring 1984, pp. 49–60; and Edwin S. Shneidman (ed.), *Endeavors in Psychology: Selections from the Personology of Henry A. Murray*, New York: Harper and Row, 1981. For an analysis of Castro's charisma, see Edward Gonzalez, *Cuba Under Castro: The Limits of Charisma*, Boston: Houghton Mifflin, 1974; and Richard Fagen, "Charismatic Authority and the Leadership of Fidel Castro," and "Mass Mobilization in Cuba: The Symbolism of Struggle," both reprinted in Rolando E. Bonachea and Nelson P. Valdés (eds.), *Cuba in Revolution*, New York: Anchor Books, Doubleday and Anchor, Inc., 1972, pp. 154–168 and 201–224, respectively.

[3] See the discussion of political time, space, and action orientations, pp. 10–13 and footnote 11, p. 11. The hubris-nemesis complex and the *niño malcriado* concept discussed below illuminate unique traits that make Castro virtually a *sui generis* case among Cubans. But these concepts may also be used to show that Castro is, in some senses, an exaggerated expression of his culture, and not just an exception to it.

we do not seek to provide a psychobiography or personality assessment of Fidel Castro; our purpose is to identify key patterns of thinking and acting that have characterized Castro as a political actor.

INTERNAL HUBRIS VERSUS EXTERNAL NEMESIS: THE TRADITIONAL DYNAMIC

Hubris is the capital sin of personal pride, a pretension to act like a god while failing to observe the established balance of man and nature. It is expressed through overweening pride, self-exaltation, arrogance, defiance, and an extreme overconfidence in one's ability and right to get away with whatever one wishes, to the point of overstepping established boundaries and disdaining the cardinal virtues of life. In ancient literature, hubris afflicted kings and conquerors who were endowed with great leadership abilities but ultimately abused their power and authority and challenged the divine order of nature to gratify their own vanity. Thus hubris is not ordinary pride—it inflates a person to exceed the fate and fortune ordained by the gods, thereby arousing their envy and angering them to restore justice and equilibrium.

Nemesis was the obscure goddess of divine retribution, righteous anger, and Olympian vengeance. Initially conceived as the personification of moral reverence for law, she evolved into a fatal deity who intervened in human affairs to restore equilibrium when it had been disturbed, usually by persons who had attained excessive power and wealth. Hubris in particular attracted Nemesis, who then humiliated and destroyed those who manifested it, often by means of terror and devastation. Thus Nemesis was a destructive force, wreaking perpetual vengeance: The battle won, she did not turn to constructive tasks of renewal.

According to the patterns of human behavior embedded in the logic of myth, one must thus beware of the ancient dynamic linking hubris and Nemesis. While the former defies proper conduct, balance, and equilibrium in human affairs, the latter violently restores them. In so doing, both have a tendency to victimize.[4]

---

[4] In ancient myths, Narcissus, Phaethon, and Icarus exemplified the traditional dynamic, though the hubris may be implied and Nemesis may be allegorical rather than personified. Aeschylus's play about Agamemnon is another kind of example. For popular accounts, see Edith Hamilton, *Mythology*, Boston, Mass.: Little, Brown, and Co., 1969, or Robert Graves, *The Greek Myths*, Baltimore, Md.: Penguin Books, 1960. For scholarly analysis, see Helen North, *Sophrosyne: Self-Knowledge and Self-Restraint in Greek Literature*, Ithaca, N.Y.: Cornell University Press, 1966. In modern parlance, the ancient terms are only occasionally used; but the dynamic is commonly expressed in sayings like "pride goeth before a fall," with the United States and Vietnam, Nixon and Watergate, and the Shah of Iran and the Islamic Revolution sometimes being paired as examples.

HUBRIS AND NEMESIS COMBINED IN THE SAME PERSON: A NEW CONCEPT

Fidel Castro, like many other powerful charismatic leaders, has often shown great hubris. He has arrogated to himself virtually all power in Cuba, he pursues grandiose ambitions as a global and regional actor, and he seeks immortality by attempting to bring down the United States. He may thus seem ripe for the fall that is conventionally presumed to be invited by such hubris.

But this way of looking at him (and others like him) ignores the fact that, in addition to having hubris, he has also internalized a self-appointed role as Nemesis: He long ago committed himself to being the nemesis, in this case, of the United States. His assumption of this role is not simply an act of hubris; it has an origin and existence that is largely independent of his hubris.

A few examples may help to clarify this concept. Many dictators have been afflicted with hubris, and many of them have fallen to a revolutionary nemesis (e.g., the Shah of Iran, Juan Perón, Anastasio Somoza). There have also been leaders who played nemesis-like roles without evincing hubris (e.g., Mahatma Ghandi, Ernesto (Che) Guevara, and Ho Chi Minh). But only a few leaders throughout history have embodied both hubris and nemesis. Castro is one; other examples may be Mohamar Khaddafi, the Ayatollah Khomeini, and Adolf Hitler.[5]

Defining Traits

In the extraordinary mindset that we have termed the "hubris-nemesis complex,"[6] the two forces coalesce to reinforce each other as compatible contradictions. Far from destroying Castro, they have so far imparted incredible energy, ambition, and dynamism.

This complex seems to form the basis for the mindsets of powerful, charismatic leaders like Castro who arrogate to themselves the right if not the duty to wreak violence and vengeance on their enemies, while imposing totalitarian rule at home and working relentlessly to expand

---

[5] A literary archetype is Captain Ahab in Herman Melville's *Moby Dick*. Castro, like other Latin American revolutionaries, has compared his sentiments to those of Don Quixote, Miguel de Cervante's fictional romantic adventurer who assumes the mission of the knight-errant and sets out to right wrongs and redress injuries. However, Don Quixote had neither the ambition for power (hubris) nor the will to vengeance (nemesis) that Castro has. Captain Ahab may be a better exemplar of many aspects of Castro and may also be instructive about the tragic, dark side of a leader in the grip of a hubris-nemesis complex.

[6] We use the term "complex" to refer to an aggregation of traits in one mindset, not as a psychological or psychiatric concept.

their power and influence abroad. (The Third World appears to have more leaders exhibiting this complex than have existed at any other time in recent memory.)

The interaction between and integration of the two forces results in something much more complex than the descriptive evidence for them seems to imply. To be as powerful as his hubris requires, Castro must fulfill his role as the nemesis of the United States; and to fulfill that role, he must possess absolute power at home and expand it abroad. Thus, the two forces, which would otherwise oppose each other, actually support each other. The stronger the one, the stronger the other; and if one force wanes, so may the other. The behavior of a leader characterized by both forces will be substantially different from that of a leader who reflects only one of them.[7]

The complex is revealed in the following distinctive traits that Castro (along with some other radical Third World leaders) constantly exhibits:[8]

---

[7]This brief formulation deals only with the hubris-nemesis complex as it may appear in some leaders. Further study may be warranted on the following aspects: (1) Though simpler words (e.g., charismatic, messianic, dogmatic, power-hungry, idealistic) could be, and often have been, used to describe Castro, the distinctiveness of the complex would not emerge. (2) The complex identifies a way of combining a set of traits that is substantially different from recognized ways such as theories about the authoritarian, the charismatic, or the narcissistic personality. (3) There are many leaders who have some of the traits of those theories but who do not evince the hubris-nemesis combination. For example, President Franklin Roosevelt was charismatic and the Shah of Iran was authoritarian and narcissistic, but neither had a hubris-nemesis complex. (4) The complex may apply not only to political leaders, but also to religious and ideological fanatics, terrorists, career criminals, and juvenile delinquents, as well as some violent schizophrenics/psychotics.

[8]Some observations relevant to a possible further elaboration of the hubris-nemesis complex with reference to terrorist leaders (which we do not consider Castro to be) are given in Post, "Dreams of Glory and the Life Cycle": "Persistent grandiose fantasies and difficulties in adapting to reality are attributes found in a number of left-wing terrorists who have been clinically interviewed. Investigations of the psychology of terrorist behavior suggest narcissistic personality structures that, while not universal, are frequently found in terrorists, particularly the 'anarchic-ideologues,' such as the Red Army Faction of West Germany and the Brigatta Rosa of Italy. Moreover, the analysis of the life course of West German terrorists indicates a pattern consistent with the background of individuals who develop narcissistic personalities. Inadequate parenting was regularly reported, and a pattern of occupational, educational, and social failure was revealed. The 'splitting' described above was very much in evidence, and the terrorists maintained an exalted view of their own capabilities, blaming the government for their failures. They had 'split off' the devalued, aggressive aspect of themselves, projected it onto the authority structure, and then justified their own aggressive anti-authority acts of political violence as being required to destroy the source of society's (and their) problems. Thus the youths who choose the path of terrorism have not been able to reconcile grandiose and unachievable dreams with their realistic limitations" (p. 53). On the less well-known Icarus complex, see Risto Fried, "The Psychology of the Terrorist," in Brian M. Jenkins (ed.), *Terrorism and Beyond: An International Conference on Terrorism and Low-Level Conflict*, The Rand Corporation, R-2714-DOE/DOJ/DOS/RC, December 1982, pp. 119–124.

A destructive-constructive messianism. He believes himself to be, and presents himself as being, a virtual messiah or savior who is on a crusade and has a fate, a destiny, or a historic mission that is both timeless and time-changing in its implications. Everything is politicized in the name of the mission and the high principles it engages.

Castro sees himself fulfilling, if not exceeding, the historical legacies of Simón Bolívar and José Martí. He also proposes to accomplish great, even monumental projects (e.g., a 10-million-ton sugar harvest, a vast housing project, a nuclear power plant). Such projects, if they are achieved, would provide evidence of practical material progress, but their purpose goes beyond that. They symbolize Castro's desire to direct vast energies at constructing something awesome that commands widespread respect and honor, thereby validating his role and fulfilling his conception of his and his nation's ultimate abilities, even as he seeks to blame and destroy his enemy for Cuba's past inabilities to live up to its hopes and its potential.

High ideals and the moralization of violence. The hubris-nemesis complex combines something great and attractive to love with something even greater and more attractive to hate. Good and evil are defined in stark, absolute, polarizing terms. Yet the leader's chosen enemy may not be seen as pure evil. Instead, the desire to humiliate and destroy the enemy may derive more from its perceived hubris (the way it has exercised its power) than from its perceived evilness.

Castro makes a deliberate effort to live up to idealized expectations and places a great emphasis on the power of ideas. Moral goals and incentives may prevail over material goals and incentives in this scheme, especially when Castro wants to appeal to new constituencies, as among Cuba's youth today. Violence is rationalized in terms of high ideals that validate the role of nemesis against the chosen enemy, and that deny any desires for material gain or glory.

Absolute power, loyalty, and attention. The complex is conducive to egocentric absolutism. Castro demands virtually absolute political power and loyalty, in a way that combines military discipline and religious devotion. This is justified as necessary to overcome fate and control destiny for a high purpose, as well as to meet potential external and internal threats.

He seeks constant attention. The bigger the audience and the larger the stage, the better. He hates to be upstaged or ignored; and if he is ignored, he may brood over how to renew his pursuit. He does not tolerate abandonment or suicide by subordinates (e.g., he was highly critical of the suicides of Haydée Santamaría and Osvaldo Dorticós),[9] and he is intolerant of rivals, both domestic and international. Domestic rivals are crushed, especially those who challenge Castro's power and goals (e.g., Huber Matos). He is more likely to compete than cooperate with international rivals (e.g., Peru's new president, Alan García), especially those whose behavior also fits the hubris-nemesis mold (e.g., Khaddafi).

He refuses to be humbled in dealings with either his enemies or his allies, even the Soviet Union. He may feign humility with selected audiences (e.g., Church representatives), and like any successful leader, he is quite capable of pragmatic decisions. But he never relents in his ambition for power or his ultimate goal of humiliating and wreaking vengeance on his chosen enemy.

A fierce sense of struggle that may become self-sacrificial. Castro believes that he can and must overcome terrible odds, threats, and obstacles. He demands that his followers put up with constant hardship, sacrifice, and struggle to achieve the goals he sets.

Defiance, rage, and vengeance (but not necessarily an all-encompassing hatred) are directed at the chosen enemy in a way that says, The more the enemy attacks us, the stronger we are. The leader with a hubris-nemesis complex thrives on confrontation and the rhetoric of threat-mongering.

He is not suicidal—indeed, he could probably endure tremendous frustration and suffering before becoming potentially suicidal. However, he is ready to take risks that expose him and his followers to death as martyrs. Under extreme circumstances (e.g., extreme frustration, a perception of extreme threat, a heightened readiness to sacrifice himself and others on behalf of his ideals, the sense of a final opportunity for victory), he might do something that risks "bringing the house down" on top of him, resulting in his death. Castro may prefer that risk, especially if it implies martyrdom and historical glory, to surrender or humiliation in his unending struggle with the United States.

This is not a definitive list. Rather, it is indicative of some basic traits that Castro exhibits that may be combined under the rubric of

---

[9]Haydée Santamaría was a co-conspirator with Castro as early as the 1953 attack on the Moncada Barracks; she was appointed head of the Casa de las Americas, Cuba's principal literary organization. Osvaldo Dorticós became President of Cuba in July 1959 and was appointed to the newly created Political Bureau of the ruling Communist Party in 1965. With the reorganization of state and government in 1976, he was appointed Minister of Justice and one of several Vice Presidents, while also retaining his Party post. The suicides of these two members of Castro's organization in the early 1980s were criticized by the regime as contrary to proper revolutionary conduct.

the hubris-nemesis complex.[10] (Preliminary research indicates that these traits may also characterize Khaddafi and Khomeini.)

Related Orientations to Political Time, Space, and Action

The defining traits of the hubris-nemesis complex concern the extraordinary drive for power and destiny and the way in which this is directed at the chosen enemy. In addition, the way in which these traits are articulated and acted out may have a lot to do with the actor's orientations toward:

1. Political time—including basic assumptions about the nature of the past, present, and future, and the calendar linking them.
2. Political space—including basic assumptions about the actor's own identity in relation to the world around him, the structure and hierarchy of power in that world, and the extent of connection and disconnection among political structures.
3. Political action—including basic assumptions about the extent to which man can affect his destiny, what constitutes legitimate action, and how best to deal with the chosen enemy.

Basic assumptions in these three dimensions may be found in any mindset, and no mindset can be analyzed fully without inquiring into all three in some form. Acting like a set of mental filters, they may be central to the translation of a particular mindset into behavior. They may affect what a person assesses is happening in the world around him, independently of his central values. And changes in a person's mindset may show up in these dimensions before they show up in the

---

[10] It is worth noting that those who exhibit this complex may have an affinity for fire symbolism. Such symbolism is important in key myths about hubris (e.g., Icarus, Phaethon, Prometheus) and in one literary portrait of the complex (Captain Ahab). Fire symbolism is also common in the behavior of radical political actors and movements that are motivated by a powerful streak of vengeance and purification (e.g., the Ku Klux Klan). Such symbolism may not be prevalent in Castro's behavior, but he has occasionally embraced it in stressful times. For example, as a child he threatened to burn down his parents' home if they kept him out of school because of bad reports about his behavior. (See the next section.) During his political imprisonment in 1953, he wondered in a letter about "men who will rise from their ashes, like the phoenix . . . ." And in another letter about the inner conflicts and struggle he was feeling, he commented: "Don't you think that such a man is consumed like a candle in the fire of its own flames?" (quoted from Carlos Franqui, *Diary of the Cuban Revolution*, New York: The Viking Press, 1980, pp. 67 and 76). Fire symbolism may not be central to Castro or to a definition of the complex, but its occasional appearance is worth noting, for it may be a further measure of the depth of Castro's commitment to violent change.

central value system.[11] The dimensions may thus help to elaborate further the hubris-nemesis complex as manifested by Castro.

Time orientation. Having a strong sense of destiny and mission, a leader with a hubris-nemesis complex, such as Castro, believes he is in tune with cosmic, invincible forces of history, and that he receives his inspiration and knowledge from a special, higher plane of philosophy and human understanding. He seeks to create a break with his nation's past and expresses an alluring, heroic vision of future salvation. In so doing, he glorifies his own past exploits in mythic terms of struggle, sacrifice, and suffering, linking himself to generations and heroes who shared his dreams. He believes he has a personal, fated mission to accomplish earth-shaking, revolutionary, even apocalyptic changes that will assure his place in history. The long-range vision of the future may seem constructive and benevolent, but it involves wreaking a great deal of vengeance and destruction to create a dramatic breakthrough to a new kind of time. This time sense is usually expressed (especially in the leader's youth) in terms of making a great leap to abruptly create a new kind of future time. But (especially later in his life) it may also concede a need for long-term struggle in which the new future emerges incrementally from changing the present. Castro regularly keeps people (individuals, groups, or the entire Cuban nation) waiting until long after the appointed time for his appearances—presumably to reflect his egocentricity and self-importance.

Space orientation. A leader with a hubris-nemesis complex sees himself as the most important object in his political horizon.[12] And this horizon is global. Believing he deserves to be world-class actor, he

---

[11]These observations about basic time, space, and action orientations are both tentative and speculative. They derive from long-term research being performed by Ronfeldt. More preliminary thought has been given to the analysis of time and space orientations than to action orientations, partly because the theoretical literature is more exhaustive on the former two than on the latter. That literature, which has barely been tapped for building frameworks with which to analyze political mindsets and world views, spans cultural anthropology (e.g., Florence and Clyde Kluckhohn, Anthony F. C. Wallace, Edward T. Hall), sociology of knowledge (e.g., Karl Mannheim, Georges Gurvitch), political philosophy (e.g., Sheldon Wolin), political geography (e.g., Alan Henrikson), child development (e.g., Jean Piaget), histories about millenialism (e.g., Norman Cohn), the concept of progress (e.g., J. B. Bury), and the idea of the future (e.g., Fred Polak), as well as the writings of advocates of violent revolution (e.g., Georges Sorel, Frantz Fanon). Early Rand research on "operational codes" (e.g., by Nathan Leites and Alexander George) derived in part from the analysis of leaders' orientations to political time and space.

[12]This aspect of Castro's spatial orientation may be linked to the psychology of narcissism. For example, see the discussion of the "mirror-hungry personality" in Jerrold M. Post, "Narcissism and the Charismatic Leader-Follower Relationship," draft, 1985, esp. pp. 4-7.

projects himself onto the world stage, seeking the limelight, commanding attention and awe.[13] (At the same time, he leads a visibly unpretentious, nonindulgent lifestyle, avoiding the materialistic consumption he associates with the hubristic decadence of the enemy.) He craves independence and an independent identity for himself and his nation. He tries to be everywhere at once, getting into every domain, including the micromanagement of minor or side issues. He seeks to cross boundaries and break barriers and will not tolerate having any built around him. He tends to interpret opportunities and constraints, successes and failures, in terms of large spatial reference factors (e.g., the "system").[14] He wants to move large pieces (e.g., the masses). And he must be keenly attentive to the centers and structures of power, especially the balance and correlation of forces around the globe. The forces that matter most are those that affect his own power and those that affect the struggle against the chosen enemy.

Action orientation. The hubris-nemesis complex is very action-oriented; it engages a powerful need to take actions to dominate and change things. This is reflected in Castro's enormous, relentless appetite for power and in his exalted sense of man's (especially his and Cuba's) ability to master destiny. As evidenced by his conduct at home, at school, at the university, and during the anti-Batista struggle, he would rather rewrite the rules of the game than follow existing

---

[13]Castro has seen to it that "internationalism" has become an increasingly important feature of Cuban policy. This may reflect a change in his beliefs about how to forge the "new Cuban man" among the Cuban masses. Ever since the late 1950s he has treated internationalism as an invaluable attribute of the committed guerrilla elites (e.g., as in the April 1959 expedition of Cuban and Panamanian guerrillas into Panama). In contrast, he initially expected that domestic struggle and achievement would suffice to raise the Cuban masses to the level of the "new Cuban man." Despite all his exhortations, the failure of the 10-million-ton sugar harvest in 1970 may have seriously disillusioned him in this regard. During the 1970s, especially with Cuba's move into Angola, he has expanded the involvement of mass elements in internationalism. Hence internationalism, which amounts to a radicalizing exposure to political spaces much larger than Cuba, has become increasingly essential to creating the "new Cuban man" and sustaining his revolutionary consciousness (see footnote 14 below).

[14]The rapid expansion of spatial horizons may be an important experience in the political formation of individuals who become radicalized and then become revolutionaries or terrorists. This kind of experience shows up in Castro's youth, when he went from the confines of a rural home to a Jesuit school in Santiago de Cuba and then to the national university in Havana. The experience also shows up in case studies of some U.S. and West European terrorists who came from rather parochial, middle-class backgrounds and then moved into big university environments. Such exposure to rapidly expanded spatial horizons surely affects thousands of students without their becoming radicalized, but this kind of experience may be important to analyzing why some individuals become radicalized while others do not.

rules, if they are not to his advantage.[15] He must lead to prevail; he cannot follow others or take their decisions for granted. He thrives on the politics of the personal, revolutionary deed that sets an example for others to follow. Indeed, he acts as though institutions are unsuited to leading the way (perhaps because they tend to be more constraint-oriented than opportunity-oriented).[16] Castro exercises his complex in Cuba through his personalistic command of decisionmaking and his totalitarian methods of rule. In his actions toward his chosen enemy abroad, he thrives on defiance and confrontation (he is strategic and not suicidal about this), and he regards compromise and accommodation as signs of weakness (though he is not above tactical retreats and concessions). He may exaggerate any sign of threat from the enemy, and he prefers military and para-military instruments. The use of force and violence, when he deems it necessary, is seen by him as clean and pure.

THE CASE OF CASTRO

Castro's version of the hubris-nemesis complex carries to an extreme two traditional tendencies in Latin American culture and politics: caudillismo, and nationalism. The *caudillo* seeks to be the all-powerful dictator who requires unquestioning loyalty and tolerates no opposition. Castro carries this to an extreme, not only by imposing totalitarian rule at home, but also by projecting himself as a global actor. In addition, the Latin American nationalist, smarting from past experiences of U.S. hegemony and intervention, is often anti-American. Even so, Castro's willfully hostile, defiant, and vengeful disposition toward the United States is rare if not unique for a powerful leader in the region.

Castro's Hubris

Ascribing hubris is a question of degree, and the dividing line between having it and not having it is imprecise. Nevertheless, by ordinary standards of behavior, and even compared to other Cuban and Latin American caudillos, Castro clearly exudes hubris. This hubris is evidenced not only in Castro's own statements and actions, but also in the observations of acquaintances who have known Castro since his youth.

---

[15]See the examples discussed in Sec. III.

[16]Thus he resisted the institutionalization of the revolution until Moscow forced it on him in the early 1970s.

By virtually all accounts, including those of former confidants who are now his enemies, Castro possesses a rare combination of leadership qualities—personal magnetism and presence, physical courage, self-confidence, determination, shrewdness, intellectual acuity, strategic vision, a sense of historical mission, and an unrelenting drive for power and recognition—that sets him apart from most other world leaders, and also from his subordinates in Cuba.[17] Through luck, perseverance, skill, and audacious, risky behavior, he has been incredibly successful at overcoming adversity, turning defeats into victories, and otherwise beating the odds over the past 30 years. Castro can thus look back on his struggle against Batista and on his 27 years of rule with considerable pride, believing that he is fulfilling the historical legacies of Simón Bolívar and José Martí.

These qualities and successes as a political leader do not in themselves amount to hubris, although they reinforce it. The tendencies to hubris show up in the ways in which he has expressed his drive for power and destiny. One of the striking continuities in Castro's life, from his youth onward, has been a determination to assert personal power that at times seems to verge on megalomania:

> He was power hungry, and the appetite grew by what it fed on. All his life he had to be Number One—the captain of his basketball team . . . or the Jefe Maximo of Cuba. He takes no advice. He brooks no opposition. Anyone who gets in his way is broken with complete ruthlessness. He is too dedicated and fanatical a revolutionary to feel gratitude or loyalty to people whose loyalty to him weakens, whatever they did for him in the past. . . . Devotion and loyalty were qualities that Fidel Castro has not only craved, but demanded. With him, it is all or nothing, for or against. There is no compromise, no middle ground.[18]

Despite his studied modesty, Castro accepts no constraints save those he chooses to impose.

The way in which Castro won his struggle against Batista in the 1950s and the way in which he and his supporters depict that struggle in heroic terms foreshadowed the hubris of the 1960s. The small attack Castro led on the Moncada Barracks on July 26, 1953, commemorated as the beginning of the Cuban Revolution, nearly proved Castro's undoing—he was captured and imprisoned. But it illustrates his penchant for setting high, seemingly unobtainable goals that he expects (and often does) achieve. The "History Will Absolve Me"

---

[17]For an excellent account, see Carlos Franqui, *Family Portrait with Fidel*, New York: Random House, 1984.

[18]From Herbert Matthews, *The Cuban Story*, New York: George Braziller, 1961, pp. 153-154.

speech that Castro wrote in prison, while remarkable for its indictment of the Batista regime, is also testimony to a proud and arrogant intelligence and to his determination to present his thoughts and actions in idealized terms:

> (M)y voice will never be drowned; for it gathers strength within my breast when I feel most alone, and it will give my heart all the warmth that cowardly souls deny me.
>
> . . .
>
> Think not that you are judging a man now, but that you shall be judged over and over again when the present shall be submitted to the crushing criticism of the future. Then, what I will have said here will often be repeated, not because I was the one who said it, but because the problem of justice is eternal.[19]

This classic speech by Castro—which he ended with the famous phrase, "Condemn me, it does not matter. History will absolve me!"—closely resembles Hitler's self-defense in court in 1924 when he was being tried on similar charges.[20]

The two-year guerrilla struggle that Castro and his small band later waged from the Sierra Maestra mountains ended almost miraculously with the sudden collapse of the Batista regime. This demonstrated to Castro that an apparently adverse correlation of forces can be overcome by the sheer will, tenacity, and skill of dedicated and resourceful revolutionaries.[21]

For a revolutionary *caudillo*, once he gains power, to undertake to remake a nation and its society is not in itself necessarily an act of hubris. But Castro expressed hubris in various specific episodes of his rule where, without any humility, he rode roughshod over institutional constraints, dismissed or ridiculed expert technical advice (often with disastrous results), and took big risks to defy the United States and even the Soviet Union. Examples of such actions in government affairs, domestic policy, and foreign policy are briefly discussed below.

---

[19]Quotes from "History Will Absolve Me (October 16, 1953)," in Rolando E. Bonachea and Nelson P. Valdés (eds.), *Revolutionary Struggle, 1947-1958: Volume 1 of the Selected Works of Fidel Castro*, Cambridge, Mass.: The MIT Press, 1972, pp. 173, 206.

[20]Hitler closed his speech by declaring: "For it is not you, gentlemen, who pass judgment on us. That judgment is spoken by the eternal court of history. . . . You may pronounce us guilty a thousand times over, but the goddess of the eternal court of history will smile and tear to tatters the brief of the state prosecutor and the sentence of this court. For she acquits us." (William L. Shirer, *The Rise and Fall of the Third Reich: A History of Nazi Germany*, New York: Simon and Schuster, 1981, p. 78.)

[21]On the importance of the "Moncada Assault Mentality" and the "Sierra Maestra Complex" for Castro's subsequent domestic and international behavior, see the discussion in the next section and Gonzalez, *Cuba Under Castro*, pp. 80-92, and 106-110.

The nature of government and the Escalante affair. The Escalante affair in 1962 consisted of a conspiracy against Castro's enormous concentration of power and the emergence of a cult of personality. In his self-defense and his attack on the conspirators, Castro included himself among those who loved the revolution beyond personal interest, vanity, and ambition. Acknowledging the seriousness of the affair, he recalled:

> Many were saying: "The cult of personality—is the same thing going to happen here as in the Soviet Union? Could the prime minister be one of those who will have to be watched to prevent his falling into the evils of the cult of personality?"

But he defended his behavior successfully by arguing that it was justified and above charges of hubris:

> We should not destroy those leaders who have prestige. What happens if we destroy them? Then, unfortunately, when difficult times come the people do not have anyone in whom to believe. . . . But this cooled the enthusiasm of the masses; this cooled the fervor of the masses.[22]

In the end, the conspirators were the ones charged with acting out of vanity, ambition, and personal interests—the very charges they had tried to level against Castro.[23]

Domestic policy and the 10-million-ton sugar harvest. Examples of hubris in Castro's domestic policies include the following:

- He launched a "revolutionary offensive" in March 1968 which eliminated much of what remained of the private sector (except for small-farm owners and independent taxi drivers) and triggered a new wave of consumer shortages and hardships, after pointedly rejecting the recommendations of his study commission. He later rebuked his "learned," "experienced," and "brainy" economists who had counseled moderation, while extolling his own "truly revolutionary science."
- In May 1969, he attacked the findings of foreign scientists at Cuba's Institute of Animal Sciences regarding how best to

---

[22]From a speech by Castro, "Against Bureaucracy and Sectarianism," in Michael Taber (ed.), *Fidel Castro, Speeches. Vol. II: Our Power Is That of the Working People*, New York: Pathfinder Press, 1983, pp. 54, 55.

[23]Though Castro successfully deflected the charges in this trial, his tendencies toward hubris reappeared in the trial of Marcos Rodríguez in 1964, where he declared: "With its little finger the power of the Revolution can fight against its enemies. . . . (W)e have made something bigger than ourselves . . . much more important than ourselves." (*Daily Report—Foreign Broadcast Information Service* (hereafter referred to as *FBIS*), April 1, 1964, p. HHHH12.)

improve milk production, disdainfully labeling the scientists "experts" and "superscientists." He countered their scientific data on the importance of corn and other feed by mustering data of his own which purportedly showed that heredity, molasses, and grass were the critical factors for production. Cuba's agro-economy was again set back.
- He insisted on pursuing the goal of a 10-million-ton sugar harvest for 1970, despite all objective evidence and the advice of his technicians that indicated such a goal was well beyond Cuba's capacity. The Cuban economy was virtually bankrupted in the harvest effort.[24]

Castro's inflated sense of his abilities in each of these areas led him to make costly mistakes. Someone who was present at one of the early meetings on economic planning reported: "Fidel . . . asked, 'Planification—isn't it like a straight jacket?' 'Yes,' someone said, 'in a sense it is.' Whereupon Castro exploded: 'Nobody is going to put *me* in a straight jacket!'"[25] His hubris proved to be his worst enemy—and in that sense, the lack of development in Cuba's domestic economy has been his nemesis.

Castro's behavior in campaigning for the calamitous 10-million-ton sugar harvest is the clearest example of his hubris in domestic policy. On a pragmatic level, the goal was part of his determination to make Cuba more independent and self-reliant. But it was a grandiose delusion that flew in the face of reality, technical advice, and even nature—all of which Castro tried to defy. In arguing that the harvest's outcome would not be determined by nature, he proclaimed

> (W)e shall take the greatest leap in the history of the world in the field of agricultural development.[26]

This leap would prove that Cuba had become a giant of a man:

> Sometimes we have said that this goal of ten million tons of sugar has made a man of our country. It has made it grow up; made it a giant.[27]

Castro intended the sugar harvest to be a giant leap not only in terms of scale and the material income it might provide, but also in

---

[24] On these and similar incidents, see Gonzalez, *Cuba Under Castro*, pp. 179ff.

[25] Reported by Herbert Matthews, *Fidel Castro*, New York: Simon & Schuster, 1969, p. 324.

[26] Castro, *FBIS*, April 22, 1968, p. O21.

[27] Castro, *FBIS*, January 3, 1966, p. HHHH4. In connection with the manhood metaphor, it may be worth noting that Castro got carried away with semen-producing bulls and the 10-million-ton sugar harvest in the same period of the late 1960s.

revolutionary conscience and spirit. For Castro, this goal seemed intended as a verification of his ability to play his role of nemesis at home and abroad:

> The question of a sugar harvest of 10 million tons has become something more than an economic goal; it is something that has been converted into a point of honor for this Revolution; it has become a yardstick by which to judge the capability of the Revolution. Our enemies have bet that we won't reach it; the microfractionists took glee in and predicted the failure of the Revolution—that is, the failure of the revolutionary line within the Revolution—with the idea that we would not reach the 10-million-ton mark, and would then have to draw in our horns, be more calm, more docile, more submissive—in short, cease being revolutionaries. And of course revolutionaries will cease to be, before ceasing to be revolutionaries![28]

While visiting the canefields at the beginning of the harvest, Castro declared that achieving the 10-million-ton figure would mean that "nothing is impossible" and "we must expect everything" to follow.[29]

A few months later, a depressed and chastened Castro, confronting a harvest of 8.5 million tons (that had massively dislocated the rest of the economy), explained the failure to achieve his goal in terms of unexpected, excessive rainfall, the inadequate milling capacity of the new "super mills," and errors in leadership.

This experience clearly did not humble Fidel. The following year he lashed out against two prominent European observers, K. S. Karol and René Dumont (both Social Democrats), who had dared to criticize his arbitrary, personalistic rule and economic dilettantism. Instead of heeding their advice and criticisms, he accused them of being CIA agents. The following year he resumed his penchant for setting grandiose, quixotic goals for domestic production, turning this time to housing construction.

Foreign policy and the 1962 missile crisis. Castro's purpose in his foreign policy extends far beyond national survival and security. He ambitiously strives to be a world-class actor who can overcome Cuba's limitations and fulfill a great ideological and strategic mission, partly through the force of his own ideas and actions, and partly by using Soviet support. In all of this, Castro has always had tremendous confidence in his own powers to assess, defy, and get away with confronting the United States.

His quest for this historic role is not simply a manifestation of megalomania. While megalomania may appear in his personality

---

[28]From a speech by Castro, March 13, 1968, as reported in Martin Kenner and James Petras (eds.), *Fidel Castro Speaks*, New York: Grove Press, Inc., 1969, p. 248.

[29]Castro, *FBIS*, January 6, 1970, p. O3.

structure, there is a basis in reality for his conviction that he can, in fact, alter the correlation of forces and the course of history:

- He has repeatedly defied the United States since coming to power, realigning Cuba with the Soviet Union and challenging "imperialism" in Latin America and elsewhere in the Third World. This feat alone establishes him as a unique historical figure; he has done what no other Latin American leader has done in this or the past century.
- He has also occasionally acted against Soviet wishes, as in his behavior during the 1962 missile crisis (discussed below), his strategy to export guerrilla warfare in the mid-1960s, and his insistence on the 10-million-ton sugar harvest. He has also led (or claimed he led) the Soviet Union into taking military initiatives that risked confrontation with the United States, as in the installation of missiles in Cuba in 1962, and the undertaking of large-scale combat operations in Angola in 1975.

As much the product of luck as adroit leadership, Castro's record of success repeatedly strengthened his proclivity to test—and even to overstep—the limits of his powers and Cuba's role in the world.

In the 1962 missile crisis, according to Carlos Franqui's eyewitness account, Khrushchev maneuvered Castro into requesting the installation of Soviet missiles on the basis of Soviet claims that the United States was preparing an invasion of Cuba. As the medium- and intermediate-range missiles began secretly arriving in Cuba in September, Castro declared that "Cuba is now ready to wage the decisive battle against the United States."[30] Then, according to Franqui's observations, Castro greatly inflated his own role, completely underestimated the U.S. reaction before and during the crisis, and greatly overestimated the Soviet commitment to Cuba:

> He seemed to have a blind belief in the Soviet military machine and shrugged off any doubts by saying that it was the Russians who were calling the tune. *He felt like one of the powerful, as if he were involved in world-changing events.* In any case, he didn't think that there would be a real conflict between the United States and the Soviet Union. And if there were an invasion, it wouldn't be his fault. Don't forget, Fidel gets his kicks from war and high tension.[31]

As the crisis unfolded, Franqui relates,

---

[30]*Bohemia* (Havana), September 7, 1962, pp. 58–59.

[31]Franqui, *Family Portrait with Fidel*, pp. 188–189 (emphasis added). Herbert Matthews, *Return to Cuba*, Hispanic American Report, Special Issue, Institute of Hispanic American and Luso-Brazilian Studies, Stanford University, 1964, p. 16, reports

I talked to Fidel about the Russians, saying that to them we were mere pawns, which they would more than willingly sacrifice to get at the United States. He was furious and accused me of pessimism and anti-Soviet prejudice. . . . He went on to say if he were in Moscow, he would send the government to the subway, which was supposed to be safe during nuclear attack, that this would be a kind of psychological attack on the Yankees.[32]

Franqui claims that Fidel gained access to a Soviet SAM installation and, through a ruse, pushed the button that shot down the U.S. U-2 reconnaissance plane then passing over Cuba.[33] (Whether Franqui actually witnessed this is unclear.) In the end, Castro was totally unprepared for and outraged by Khrushchev's orders for the withdrawal of the missiles, which he saw as a Soviet abandonment of Cuba.[34]

The point here is not that Castro made a miscalculation; any leader may do that. But his behavior in the missile crisis revealed an inflated sense of power and pride about being involved in an earthshaking event.

Recent Foreign Policy Behavior. During 1975–76, Castro dispatched 36,000 Cuban troops to Angola to help consolidate a Marxist-Leninist regime there. During a triumphant one-month tour of African states in 1977, Castro declared presumptuously that "Africa is the weakest link in the imperialist chain today. . . . There are excellent perspectives there for going directly from tribalism to socialism."[35]

But in 1983, Castro misjudged the extent to which he could influence events on the island of Grenada.[36] Cuba and the Soviet Union evidently shared a strategic interest in converting Grenada into a mutual ally and potential military position. However, Castro was unable to prevent the power struggle within the New Jewel Movement that led to the death of his protégé, Maurice Bishop, nor was he able to ensure that Moscow would not favor Bernard Coard over Bishop. He

---

a talk with Castro in which he disputed accounts that the Soviets initiated the idea to install the missiles. "Then he said, and during our 15-minute conversation he repeated it emphatically at least four times: '*Fuimos nosotros que hemos planteado la idea de los misiles.*' ('We were the ones who put forward the idea of the missiles.')"

[32]Franqui, *Family Portrait with Fidel*, p. 192.

[33]Ibid., p. 193.

[34]Castro was by no means restrained in his criticism of the Soviets: "'Son of a bitch! Bastard! Asshole!' Fidel went on in that vein for quite some time. The Russians had abandoned us, made a deal with the Americans, and never bothered to inform us. Fidel had no idea." (Franqui, *Family Portrait with Fidel*, p. 194.)

[35]Interview for *Afrique-Asie*, published in *Granma Weekly Review*, May 22, 1977, p. 2.

[36]For an analysis of the Grenada affair based on captured documents, see Jiri and Virginia Valenta, "Leninism in Grenada," *Problems of Communism*, July-August 1984, pp. 1–23.

was powerless to deter or oppose the U.S.-led intervention. And once again Moscow abandoned Castro militarily. The result was a stunning defeat for Castro's foreign policy in the Caribbean Basin, strains in the Cuban-Soviet relationship to a degree unmatched since the late 1960s, and a sudden feeling of vulnerability to a resurgence of U.S. power.[37]

Far less is known about Castro's thoughts and actions in the Grenada affair than about his behavior in the 1962 missile crisis, and years may pass before much is known. Nonetheless, the familiar pattern of ambition, pride, arrogance, and overconfidence apparently remains in place, though it is perhaps somewhat tempered.

A residue of hubris also appeared in a recent affair involving a breakthrough in negotiations with the United States. Castro apparently believed he had reached a *quid pro quo* with the United States by authorizing the December 14, 1984, migration agreement whereby Cuba agreed to the return of the "undesirable" Cubans residing in the United States and to other forms of regulated migration between the two countries. Castro apparently expected that the Reagan administration in return would adopt a less hostile overall policy toward Cuba, and even Nicaragua. The migration agreement occurred at a time of virtual war hysteria in Cuba, but Castro justified the surprising turn of events to the Cuban people by claiming that the agreement ended 26 years of abnormal relations between the two countries. He said it derived from positive changes in U.S. policy (e.g., the arrest and conviction of a Cuban exile leader), and he took credit for helping to achieve those changes.[38] Then, evidently believing he had softened U.S. policy, he relaxed island defenses and gave a series of interviews distinguished by their moderate tone. However, to his surprise and anger, Radio Martí began to broadcast in May 1985.[39] Castro reacted by immediately suspending the migration agreement.[40]

This episode is so recent that little is known about Castro's thoughts and actions. And of course it is not unusual for a leader to believe he has negotiated a *quid pro quo* and then be outraged when it fails to take effect according to his expectations. That is not hubris. The hubris in this episode appears in Castro's apparent ambition and

---

[37]See Edward Gonzalez, "The Cuban and Soviet Challenge in the Caribbean Basin," *Orbis*, Spring 1985, pp. 73–94.

[38]The televised speech appears in *Granma Weekly Review*, December 23, 1984, esp. pp. 5–6. Immediately after the speech, Castro sought out a U.S. diplomat to impress upon him the extent to which he (Castro) had adopted a moral position and made a "personal commitment" to the American people in negotiating the agreement.

[39]Prolonged delays in starting the Radio Martí broadcasts may also have strengthened Castro's delusions that he had stymied U.S. policy once again.

[40]He also rescinded the 1979 agreement whereby Cuban-Americans could visit their families on the island.

idealized conviction that a minor concessionary agreement on his part would lead to a big breakthrough with the United States. This time, his exalted view of his power and influence did not bear fruit.

Finally, in his self-appointed role as the key spokesman of Latin America and the Third World in general, Castro has been quite intolerant of rivals. For example, although Cuba has occasionally collaborated with militantly anti-U.S. Third World countries such as Iran, Libya, and Vietnam to supply arms to insurgents abroad,[41] Castro's self-image as the greatest revolutionary leader of the Third World keeps him from personally collaborating with other candidates for that position. He resents being upstaged or subordinated. Thus, although he has not been openly critical of leaders like Khaddafi or Khomeini, Castro has apparently not tried to coordinate strategy with them against the United States. He may harbor a personal resentment against Khaddafi in particular, and may have resented Khaddafi's assistance roles in Nicaragua and elsewhere in the Caribbean Basin.[42] Castro's sensitivities on this score were reflected in his bitterness toward Peru's youthful new president, Alan García, who in 1985 called for approaching debt and other hemispheric issues in ways that are left-leaning but repudiate Castro's hardline radicalism.[43]

Intellectualism and the Denial of Hubris

Like other leaders who may have a hubris-nemesis complex, Castro expresses his ambition and his idealism not simply through dictatorial behavior, but also as a quasi-intellectual committed to grasping and dispensing knowledge. Indeed, he has a strong didactic compulsion to

---

[41]These various suppliers may end up preferring to supply different insurgent groups within the target country because of substantial tactical and strategic differences over how the insurgency should be prosecuted and which groups deserve the most support.

[42]Castro was snubbed by Khaddafi at the meeting of the Non-Aligned Movement in Algeria in 1973, where they met for the first time. Later, during Castro's 1977 tour through Africa, he was angered when Khaddafi met him at an obscure location in the interior of Libya rather than at the airport in Tripoli. The potential for rivalry, even animosity, may be reflected in recent, unsubstantiated press reports in January 1986 that Cuba was concerned Libya might be plotting to create a crisis in Central America (e.g., at the Panama Canal) that would be blamed on Cuba, thereby distracting the United States from punishing Khaddafi for his support of terrorist actions in the Middle East and Europe.

[43]In addition to opposing Castro's call for an end to debt payments, García indicated that Castro was acting irresponsibly in trying to blame the international economy for the debt problem, turn the debt into an East-West issue, and "struggle against one dependency with the weapons of another dependency." García also implied that Castro was too "messianic." Castro's ire was first aroused by a press conference García gave on July 19, 1985. The quotes above come from García's address to the UN General Assembly in New York, September 23, 1985, as reported in FBIS, September 26, 1985, esp. pp. J5–J6.

discourse on diverse subjects, both in large assemblies and in interviews. Today, as in the 1960s, he seeks to demonstrate his mastery not only of politics and economics, but also of complex, highly technical subjects.

This pattern is partly the result of his intelligence. He has a thirst for knowledge and an impressive capacity for quick study. As demonstrated by his acquired, but unschooled and unscientific, knowledge of agronomy, Castro's mistaken insistence on grass feeding in 1968 was strengthened by the brief, tragic visit in December 1964 of an obscure French agronomist, André Voisin, whom Castro had personally invited to Cuba. Voisin was scheduled to give a series of lectures on how to nourish Cuba's dairy herds on pasture grass rather than imported feed, but he died before the end of his visit. Following Voisin's first lecture, Castro took the podium for nearly two hours, giving "one of his frequent demonstrations of sheer brain power. . . . Even Voisin was enthralled, exclaiming that Fidel was his best student and that he could not understand how a Prime Minister . . . could manage to master such a complex technical subject in so short a time."[44]

Castro's ability to intellectualize and idealize reflects not only his innate intelligence, but also his lengthy Jesuit training. Before taking his law degree at the University of Havana, Castro attended Jesuit schools in Santiago de Cuba and Havana for 12 years. His Jesuit education was an important formative experience that would help set him apart from most other Cubans:

> The Society of Jesus encourages freedom of thought more than any other order of the Catholic Church. It is quite political and the most radical on either extreme of the religious orders. . . . They [the Jesuits] prize eloquence, self-discipline and knowledge above all, while eschewing sensuality and materialism. Stress is put on the intellect rather than the emotions, on the universal rather than the particular, which accounts for a certain ruthless quality.[45]

Today, decades later, Castro continues to be the didactic, all-knowing, authoritative leader who can expound articulately on a wide range of issues. He continues to venture into specialized technical areas. While addressing more than 1,000 delegates from 40 countries at an orthopedic congress held in Havana last June, he conceded that he was "not a specialist in orthopedics," then went on to claim,

---

[44]Maurice Halperin, *The Taming of Fidel Castro*, University of California Press, 1981, pp. 136–137.
[45]Gene Vier, "Analyzing Fidel," *Human Behavior*, July 1975, pp. 66–67.

> I am very much in contact with our doctors and, naturally, I've become familiar with some medical terms and specific concepts. And there are also the books I read and certain scientific principles. Perhaps I had a vocation for medicine, but was unaware of it.[46]

Three months later, at a press forum on Latin America's financial situation, he posed as an authority on the econometrics of the debt crisis. To prove the impossibility of repayment, he showed how he had analyzed the issue from "the economic and mathematical point of view," apparently using computers to make calculations that rested on his "many analyses, several formulas, and variants."[47]

As these and countless other statements suggest, he is compelled to demonstrate his intellectual prowess and to have his authoritativeness recognized. The editors of Castro's March 1985 *Playboy* interview noted that his answers "are ten, 15, 20 minutes long, and follow-ups become academic. He waves away interruptions as his answers pile on one another."[48]

It is typical of Castro that he denies having hubris by claiming that he never sought to gain power, that the revolution does not belong to him, and that he has made mistakes in the past. In accordance with his Jesuit background, Castro insists on his modesty and nobility of purpose, much in the manner of a stoic priest. He expressed his views about this while imprisoned in 1955:

> The more I come to depend on life's comforts and forget that I can be perfectly happy not owning anything, the lower I slip in my own estimation. That's how I have learned to live, and it makes me more fear-inspiring as a passionate defender of an ideal that has been reaffirmed and strengthened by sacrifice. . . . Since I have been here, my biggest struggle has been to insist and never tire of insisting that I don't need anything; I have needed only books and they should be thought of as spiritual possessions.
>
> . . .
>
> I can't have any weaknesses; no matter how small they might be today, you would never be able to count on me tomorrow.[49]

And he continues to think this way today:

> You will not see a statue of me anywhere, nor a school with my name, nor a street, nor little town, nor any type of personality cult, because we have not people to believe, but to think.[50]

---

[46]*Granma Weekly Review*, June 30, 1985, p. 2.
[47]From *FBIS*, September 20, 1985, esp. pp. Q6–Q7.
[48]"Playboy Interview: Fidel Castro," *Playboy*, August 1985, p. 57.
[49]In Franqui, *Diary of the Cuban Revolution*, p. 88.
[50]Transcript, MacNeil/Lehrer News Hour, PBS, February 12, 1985, p. 2.

> Money does not motivate me. . . . Likewise, the lust for glory, fame and prestige does not motivate me. I really think that ideas motivate me. Ideas, conviction, are what spur a man to struggle in the first place. . . . I think that personal selflessness grows; the spirit of sacrifice grows; you gradually relinquish personal pride, vanity . . . all those elements that in one way or another exist in all men.
>
> . . .
>
> If you do not guard against those vanities, if you let yourself become conceited or think that you are irreplaceable or indispensable, you can become infatuated with all of that—the riches, the glory. I've been on guard against those things.[51]

Thus even though Castro denies that he is afflicted with hubris, he admits he must be on guard against its lure.

This deliberate denial of behavior that might otherwise be typical of the conqueror or dictator may be related to Castro's dedication to being the nemesis of the United States. By leading a visibly spartan, unpretentious, nonindulgent lifestyle, he avoids, indeed shuns, the materialistic consumption that he, like others with a hubris-nemesis complex, associates with the perceived hubris and decadence of his chosen enemy.

Evidence of Nemesis in Castro

Castro's nemesis-like behavior appears first of all toward the United States, and second toward the old Cuba. His bitterest feelings of vengeance and justice have always been directed at the United States, however, because in his view its godlike presumptions and actions are the epitome of hubris and thus deserve his wrath. In contrast, the old Cuban society was simply rotten and evil; also, it did not prove to be an enduring enemy.

Compared with documenting Castro's hubris, which is evident mainly in his miscalculations and errors, it is much easier to document his conception of himself as the nemesis of the United States. During his early twenties, Castro identified his destiny with fulfilling the legacies left by Simón Bolívar and José Martí:

> I was quixotic, romantic, a dreamer, with very little political knowhow but with a tremendous thirst for knowledge and a great impatience for action. I could not yet foresee distinctly the great enemies I would have to fight, but I was already beginning to detect them. The dreams of Martí and Bolívar, as well as a kind of utopian socialism, were vaguely stirring within me.

---

[51]"Playboy Interview," pp. 58–59.

> I came to realize more and more clearly that the policy of the United States, and its wholly disproportionate development with respect to Latin America, was the great enemy of the unification and development of the Latin American nations; the United States would always do its utmost to maintain the weakness and division on which is based its policy of directing the fate of our peoples as it pleased.[52]

Thus years before launching his anti-Batista struggle in 1953, Castro was possessed by a growing hatred and rage toward the United States.[53]

The more he focused on holding the United States responsible for Cuba's and Latin America's plight, the more he realized that his all-consuming mission would be to make the Cuban Revolution the nearby nemesis of the United States, and the avenging, wrathful goddess of retributive justice in the Americas. Thus while fighting as a guerrilla in the Sierra Maestra, Castro wrote Celia Sanchez in June 1958:

> When I saw rockets firing . . . I swore to myself that the North Americans were going to pay dearly for what they were doing. When this war is over a much wider and bigger war will commence for me: the war I am going to wage against them. I am aware that this is my true destiny.[54]

Befitting the adoption of a nemesis role, Castro then began to express more clearly his view that the United States was guilty of hubris in its behavior toward Cuba and Latin America—a view that was evident in his reactions to his meetings with Vice President Richard Nixon and Ambassador Philip Bonsal:

---

[52]Franqui, *Diary of the Cuban Revolution*, p. 9.

[53]Some observers link this hatred to Castro's relations with his father. According to Rufo López-Fresquet, *My Fourteen Months with Castro*, Cleveland: The World Publishing Company, 1966, p. 166, "Castro has always been motivated by hate. He hates the existing society, which made him suffer for his family origins. He hates the economic structure, symbolized by a rich father who never gave him affection. He hates the U.S., which he saw during his childhood in the form of the oppressive American sugar-estate managers." According to Hugh Thomas, *Cuba: The Pursuit of Freedom*, New York: Harper and Row, 1971, pp. 803–805, Fidel Castro's father, who originally came to Cuba from Spain, "always had a violent hispanic antipathy toward the North Americans, who he thought, rightly, had cheated the Spaniards out of victory over the Cuban rebels: an odd origin, but no doubt genuine, for his son's similarly hispanic dislike of the Monster of the North." The Castro family lived in a region that was among the most "dominated by the North American presence." Indeed, the father became wealthy in part through dealings with the United Fruit Company. Information about Castro's relations with his father remains open to question, however. For example, Castro recently observed that in some respects his father was "a profoundly decent man" who often helped poor sugar cane workers sustain their lives between harvests, and thus treated those workers better than did the nearby U.S.-run estates. (Translated from *Fidel e a Religiao: Conversas com Frei Betto*, São Paulo, 1985.)

[54]Bonachea and Valdés (eds.), *Revolutionary Struggle*, p. 379.

You ought to have heard the conversations with Ambassador Bonsal from the beginning. . . . He lectured me, criticized us and our Revolution, complained, threatened. There was never the slightest understanding of the Revolution or sympathy with what we were trying to do. I can assure you I felt humiliated as a Cuban at the way I, the Prime Minister of Cuba, was being talked to. This was not the attitude of two friendly nations of the OAS. This was an effort at dictation, direction and complaint. You ought, also, to hear how the Soviet representatives talk. They are friendly, respectful, sympathetic, understanding. They make us feel like a sovereign country. The United States Ambassador tries to make us feel as if we must do what the United States wants.[55]

His growing accusations thus helped justify his rejection and defiance of the United States and his switch to a pro-Soviet alliance.[56]

To be sure, the dynamics of the hubris-nemesis complex may not explain Castro's embrace of Marxism-Leninism and the Soviet Union, but they are inherent in his conception of his ideological and strategic mission. Early in life he acquired anti-capitalist, anti-U.S., and pro-socialist biases that may have derived as much from Jesuit as from Marxist influences.[57] Castro's embrace of Marxism-Leninism and the Soviet Union soon after taking power has often been interpreted as an unmasking of the real Castro (who was allegedly a Communist all along), as a tactical move to secure a Soviet commitment to Cuba, and as a reaction to U.S. pressure. Yet it is clear from this analysis that, apart from ideology and strategy, Castro was resolved from the outset to eradicate the U.S. presence from Cuba and to lead a vengeful anti-imperialist struggle in the hemisphere.[58] Thus, as early Castro confidante Teresa Casuso observed after going into exile, "His obsession with destruction, hatred, and retaliation would select communism as the system best suited to accommodate him."[59]

---

[55]López-Fresquet, *My Fourteen Months with Castro*, p. 26. The same source also reports (p. 169) on Castro's anger following his meeting with Nixon in April 1959 in the United States: "Castro was angry. He swore and added, 'This man has spent the whole time scolding me.'"

[56]Castro has of course denied that he was pushed into socialism; he claimed instead that U.S. actions only accelerated the process he had in mind.

[57]It is possible that if Castro had matured in the 1930s instead of the 1950s, he would have admired Fascism in his desire to amplify his power and be the nemesis of the United States. (See Vier, "Analyzing Fidel," passim.)

[58]The conventional wisdom, especially among sympathizers of Castro and critics of U.S. policy toward Cuba, that U.S. threats and pressures against Cuba explain his behavior ignores Castro's own nature and ambitious political agenda.

[59]She also believed Castro was not a Communist before 1959 and was "pushed into its arms." (From Teresa Casuso, *Cuba and Castro*, New York: Random House, 1961, p. 160.) She saw Fidel as "resembling several characters from Greek literature. When he plants himself like a predestined exterminator, he is Orestes. When, like a crazed man, he rushes against non-existent enemy armies visible only to his warped mind, he is the

As distance and hostility grew between Cuba and the United States, Castro's views hardened. In 1966, he declared:

> (T)he last nation—hear this well—that the last nation on earth which for infinite historic, geographic, patriotic, revolutionary, and moral reasons, the last nation to make peace with imperialism will be this country![60]

He repeated this vow in 1968, at a time when Soviet-Cuban relations were strained, economic shortages were growing, and rumors were circulating that Havana and Washington might enter into exploratory talks:

> Never, under any circumstances—and the comrades of our Central Committee know this; they know this is the line adopted by our Committee—never, under any circumstance, even in the most difficult circumstances, will this country approach the imperialist Government of the United States—not even should it one day place us in the situation of having to choose between the continued existence of the Revolution or such a step. Because, gentlemen, that would be the moment at which the Revolution would have ceased to exist.[61]

Castro has constantly drawn strength from the U.S. blockade and other threats he has defied since coming to power, including various assassination attempts:

> (E)very action by our enemies has contributed to the creation in our people of virtue and strength. . . . (W)ithout the implacable and criminal blockade unleashed by the imperialists against us, we would not have this revolutionary spirit of the people today.[62]

Indeed, this theme—that U.S. attacks and threats strengthen virtue, resolve, and dedication to the revolution—has become a permanent fixture in Castro's mindset. Castro implicitly acknowledges that his tendencies toward hubris and nemesis inspire each other when he argues that

---

tragic Ajax, the impressive and touching warrior blinded by the gods. But the one he most closely resembles in his best moments is Odysseus, with all his sly tricks, his daring, his valor, his weaknesses. But Fidel has at least one weakness that Homer spared his hero: he wants to be a god, whereas Odysseus, when he had the opportunity to be one, had the greatness to prefer to go on being a man. It is this difference that as a human being elevates Odysseus and condemns Fidel Castro." (Ibid., pp. 187–188.)

[60]Castro, *FBIS*, January 3, 1966, p. HHHH4.

[61]*Granma Weekly Review*, August 25, 1968, p. 4. See Gonzalez, *Cuba Under Castro*, p. 78 and passim.

[62]Castro, *FBIS*, April 22, 1968, pp. O4–5.

These marvels have risen from difficulty and new marvels will rise, more each day. And from the great goals we set ourselves, which we are forced to set partly through the fault of imperialism.[63]

The Death-Defying Face of Nemesis

Throughout his term in power, Castro has shown a readiness to risk death, both his own and others', in his fight against the United States,[64] sometimes reflecting a *Gotterdammerung* tendency in his hubris.[65]

In 1959, after his fellow cabinet members warned him that his intention to oust Manuel Urrutia, the first post-revolutionary president, could create a constitutional crisis and even open the way for a U.S. invasion, Castro declared:

> That does not matter to me, because if they send the marines and kill three to four hundred thousand Cubans, they will build a monument to me bigger than the one for José Martí.[66]

Two years later, Castro did not hesitate to climb into a tank and head for the Bay of Pigs to combat the exiles' military invasion. More recently, he reacted to the U.S.-led intervention in Grenada by ordering the small Cuban contingents of armed workers there to fight to the end, without reinforcements.[67]

---

[63]Castro, *FBIS*, January 31, 1969, p. O11.

[64]Castro apparently enjoyed defying death even as a child. According to José Pardo Llada, "Fidel: De los Jesuitas al Moncada," *Enciclopedia Popular Ilustrada*, Bogotá, Colombia: Editores Colombia, Ltd., 1976, pp. 8–9, he used to play a game that began by walking out on railroad tracks on a bridge at a fatal height above a river. When a train arrived, he would jump down and dangle between the tracks, hanging onto a cross-tie while the trained passed overhead.

[65]Casuso, *Cuba and Castro*, p. 188, observed, "One thing is certain: Fidel lives in tremendous tension. He is a wreckage of conflicts and contradictions. It is not for nothing that his first speech, in the hour of victory, was haunted with references to death, and that Cuba has been soaked with the tragedy-laden slogan *patria o muerte* (fatherland or death)." Thomas, *Cuba: The Pursuit of Freedom*, p. 1055, however, suggests that this and related slogans simply echoed those of the Spanish Risorgimento and the Cuban War of Independence.

[66]Castro, in a cabinet meeting in July 1959, as reported by Ernesto Betancourt (interview with Edward Gonzalez, October 3, 1985).

[67]The Cuban military officers on Grenada surrendered or sought refuge in the Soviet embassy, thereby incurring Castro's wrath. Castro's order to fight to the end was surely sacrificial, but it was not necessarily irrational: He may have hoped that a handful of U.S. casualties would resurrect the Vietnam syndrome, making the United States more reluctant to take military action next against Nicaragua, or possibly Cuba. Thus an act that initially seemed irrational to many outside observers may, according to a different set of criteria, have contained a strong element of rationality.

Castro's defiance and feeling of invincibility against even a massive U.S. attack appeared again in his belief that his "Peoples' War" campaign and the organization of the Territorial Troop Militia (MTT) "have created the conditions which enable us to feel that we are invincible."[68] Castro does not hesitate to defy even the prospect of nuclear annihilation. In proclaiming that there was little the United States could do against Cuba, he declared in June 1985:

> What can they do, drop three nuclear bombs here? No, they can't do that. Besides, they know we aren't afraid of their three nuclear bombs, which is even more important. Three nuclear bombs or 100, 1,000, or 10,000 nuclear bombs amount to something if you're afraid of them, but if you aren't they're chicken excrement, that's all.[69]

DEVELOPMENT AND DURABILITY OF THE COMPLEX

As an analytical construct, the hubris-nemesis complex seems to provide a useful way of illuminating a combination of key traits exhibited by Castro and other militantly anti-U.S. revolutionary leaders. These traits lie at the core of Castro's mindset.

This does not necessarily mean that all aspects of Castro's mindset can be subsumed under this complex, nor does it explain his political behavior under all circumstances. For example, he has repeatedly demonstrated great leadership ability and that may explain his responses in some situations. Nevertheless, there is convincing evidence that the dynamics of hubris and nemesis have played central roles in his thoughts and actions since childhood and will continue to do so.

A person is not simply born with this complex; it may take years and years to develop and take hold. In Castro's case, the hubris-related traits developed first. The nemesis-related traits were apparent in some early actions toward his parents, guardians, teachers, and childhood rivals, but he did not develop a nemesis-like focus until he began his revolutionary guerrilla struggle against the Batista regime.

Because a desire for vengeance—along with all the passions and purposes that desire may arouse—is so central to the complex, the origin of the nemesis dimension may be traceable to a deep wound or abiding injury to the individual's identity and sense of justice.[70] It may not

---

[68]*Granma Weekly Review*, June 9, 1985, p. 3.

[69]*Granma Weekly Review*, June 16, 1985, p. 6.

[70]Revenge is a concept found in all cultures, but it seems to be especially prevalent in Arab and Latin cultures, perhaps in part because of the great importance these cultures place on pride, dignity, honor, and respect, and their relation to justice and injustice.

matter whether the injury is to the person, the family, the society, or the nation, so long as it is taken very personally, perhaps especially during the formative years of childhood and youth. The related development of the hubris dimension, and hence of the full complex, may then follow from the ability of a leader to achieve recurrent triumphs by exploiting, at least some of the time, his and others' sense of wounded pride and craving for revenge.

Once nurtured, the hubris-nemesis complex may prove very durable over time, as long as the bearer regularly receives some (even slight) reinforcement through the turn of events and holds some (even slight) hope of fulfilling his dreams and ambitions.[71] No matter what Castro's tack may be at any particular time, it is fundamental, ingrained, and ever-present in his mindset. He may never relinquish his dual desires to be godlike and to harm the United States. The complex may at times be subordinated to some expedient, pragmatic requirement of the moment, but it would be an error to view Castro as just another pragmatic leader who will make conventional cost-benefit calculations of his interests. His mindset is geared to resisting rather than responding to U.S. economic inducements or military threats, or to a combination of them.

Indeed, Castro has revealed as much in his reflections on his early training in Jesuit schools where "the main argument they use is reward or punishment." In his view, political as well as religious beliefs and actions should depend on faith and conviction, "understandable reasons and on the intrinsic value of what is done."

> (I)n my opinion, that which is done through fear of punishment or in hopes of reward is not entirely generous, not totally worthy, and does not deserve praise, admiration, or respect.[72]

---

[71]In analyzing the effects of narcissism, which may be related to the concept discussed here, Post, "Dreams of Glory and the Life Cycle," provides a strong case (pp. 58–59) that "the end of life through old age or the advent of serious illness may be particularly threatening to narcissistic leaders with messianic goals. For some, it may lead to an increased urgency to accomplish these goals before their time is up. For others, narcissistic omnipotence may contribute to denial of their own mortality. It is important to emphasize that for talented individuals with self-confidence, actions in pursuit of dreams may be highly creative and have extremely positive consequences. But when there is a significant gap between the dreams of glory and the dry ashes of reality, radical changes in ideology or precipitous actions can occur which historians later come to record as tragic." Castro indicates he may be sensitive about this when he claims, "I could tell you that in the case of Cuba our accomplishments exceed our dreams and we have achieved, not a utopian phase but a subutopian phase, that is, in our dreams we were short of Utopia and beyond it in our accomplishments." (Translated from *Fidel e a Religiao: Conversas com Frei Betto.*)

[72]Ibid.

Fidel equates this kind of conviction with the ability to become a religious martyr or a revolutionary hero.[73]

Thus there is no possibility of any compromise or accommodation with the United States on core issues. This helps to explain why he embarked upon his military adventures in Angola and Ethiopia precisely when the Ford and Carter administrations were actively seeking a more normalized relationship with Cuba. It also means that he would be unlikely to accept a Cuban-U.S. accommodation even if that were the only way to ensure the survival of his regime, his military personnel/advisers in Nicaragua, or his troops in Angola.[74]

Committed from the outset to fulfilling his anti-American destiny, Castro remains ready to put Cuba at risk for his own purposes. In the short term, however, he is capable of calculated pragmatic behavior that feigns moderation and preserves his power before he returns to advancing his grand long-term ambitions.

---

[73]Further research may show that most leaders with a hubris-nemesis complex have died a violent death, and that none has ever given up the complex.

[74]It is unlikely that Castro will one day become sufficiently tired and disillusioned to retire from public life. It is conceivable, however, that following a period of inability to pursue his maximalist goals, he might forsake ordinary politics to become a radical religious leader—perhaps emulating Ignatius Loyola, who was a soldier for much of his life and then became a priest and founded the Jesuit order. If this happened, it is likely that Castro's hubris-nemesis complex would persist and would be expressed in a different form. For some of Castro's views on religion, see the discussion in Sec. V below.

III. CASTRO'S *MODUS OPERANDI*

Charismatic leaders imbued with a hubris-nemesis complex have unique personality and behavioral characteristics that make them highly attractive to their followers and effective as leaders. As charismatic personalities, they become virtual demigods to their supporters. Their charismatic authority is renewed when their political behavior proves unusually effective in helping them expand their political power, pursue grandiose objectives, and outwit domestic or international foes.[1] Adolf Hitler was a prime example, until his catastrophic defeat at Stalingrad in 1942 first damaged his leadership image. With his own unique personality and behavior, Castro has thus far operated successfully on both the domestic and international fronts.

This section looks at facets of Castro's personality that relate to his charismatic attraction and exercise of political power as a *caudillistic* leader. Five broad behavioral patterns are identified that recur throughout his political career and characterize his *modus operandi* as a political actor, particularly in dealing with adversaries: *violence-prone rebelliousness, deceitfulness, radicalism, strategic opportunism,* and *tactical pragmatism*. The first two can be traced directly to his childhood; the remaining three, to his revolutionary experiences. The section assesses whether Castro's international behavior has changed in recent years, and which of his modes of behavior are likely to predominate in his future policies.

The analysis that follows is not intended as a psychoanalytic portrait of Castro as an individual. Its intent is, rather, to bring into sharper focus Castro's personality traits as a *political actor* and to examine his *modus operandi* against antagonists.

THE CHARISMATIC *CAUDILLO*

Ever since he came to power in 1959, Castro's public image has been that of an appealing, engaging, and accessible political leader who

---

[1] According to Max Weber's classic formulation, success is essential to the maintenance of charismatic authority: "The charismatic leader gains and maintains authority solely by proving his strength in life. If he wants to be a prophet, he must perform miracles; if he wants to be a war lord, he must perform heroic deeds. Above all, however, his divine mission must prove itself in that those who faithfully surrender to him must fare well. If they do not fare well, he is obviously not the master sent by the gods." (H. H. Gerth and C. Wright Mills (eds.), *From Max Weber: Essays in Sociology*, New York: Oxford University Press, 1958, p. 249.)

enjoys the warm support and admiration of his people. His leadership qualities and personal magnetism are undoubtedly genuine and not the product of clever image-making. Thus, he is able to hold audiences, large or small, by the very force of his personality, the passion of his convictions, and the intellectual command that he seems to wield over virtually any topic. Even today, he attracts legions of admirers both outside and inside Cuba, including foreign intellectuals, politicians, journalists, and even clergymen.

The power and attraction of Castro's personality was evident long before his stunning defeat of Batista imbued him with charismatic authority. In the early days of the revolutionary struggle, beginning with his 1953 attack on the Moncada Barracks, he was able to enlist devoted supporters in his cause, despite the overwhelming odds and personal danger and hardships they faced. These men and women— the *Moncadistas* and the Sierra Maestra guerrilla veterans—have since constituted the *fidelistas*, the core of the regime, and have remained Castro's most loyal supporters.

The many sides of Castro's personality have enabled him to attract many different types of followers. He is a man of action, endowed with impressive physical stature, courage, and audacity; he is also a leader with superior intelligence, singular determination, and strategic vision. The faithful thus include not only revolutionary activists, but also intellectuals and idealists of moderate as well as radical persuasions.[2] Whatever their motives, they accepted Castro long ago as their *líder máximo*.

Others, however, eventually became repelled by the darker (and less public) side of Castro's personality—the megalomania, *caudillismo*, radicalism, and totalitarian drive which he had so ably concealed prior to 1959. Unlike those who remained in the regime, this group was able to accept him as a leader but not as a despotic *caudillo*, however remarkable his talents. At bottom, their differences with Castro may not have revolved around his own well-defined, systematic "ideology" because he had none, except for his radical anti-capitalist propensities and his insistence on complete power and subordination.[3] The course of the Cuban revolution is thus strewn with the wreckage of former co-

---

[2] Castro's attractiveness to a wide assortment of men and women is remarked on by former followers Teresa Casuso, in *Cuba and Castro*, and Mario Llerena, in *The Unsuspected Revolution*, Ithaca: Cornell University Press, 1978.

[3] "Castroism is a leader in search of a movement, a movement in search of power, and power in search of ideology.... Castro's ideology has never come out of himself. He has only produced a 'road to power,' which has attached itself to different ideologies. He won power with one ideology and has held it with another.... Castro did not have an ideological core of his own." (Theodore Draper, *Castroism: Theory and Practice*, New York: Praeger, 1965, pp. 44–48.)

conspirators, revolutionary fighters, political allies, and even family members who broke with or were destroyed by Castro—among them, Mario Llerena, Manuel Urrutia, Huber Matos, Teresa Casuso, Felipe Pazos, Juanita Castro, and Carlos Franqui.

Yet, many of the traits that repelled those followers are precisely the ones that have helped Castro deal effectively with adversaries, both individuals and nation-states. His drive for power, single-minded purposefulness, cunning, and mendacity, are shared in varying degrees with other ruthless *caudillistic* leaders, such as Franco, Perón, and Batista. But he differs from other *caudillos* in that his hubris-nemesis complex involves a messianic purpose and drive that the others lacked.

In his pursuit of power and the fulfillment of his destiny, Castro has exhibited a highly individualized mode of political behavior for dealing with his adversaries at home and abroad. The behavioral patterns and traits that comprise this *modus operandi* are not confined to single instances but recur constantly. While some accounts of Castro's behavior may be incomplete and distorted, the pattern (often described in Castro's own accounts) recurs with too much frequency to be dismissed.[4]

Castro's *modus operandi* toward adversaries, both real and potential, can be traced back to his childhood, when he was able to manipulate his parents, guardians, and grade school teachers and to assert his dominance over other students. His idiosyncratic behavior was reinforced and broadened in his later political career, especially as he gained experience—and successes. The result is a unique pattern of political behavior that has remained remarkably constant over time.[5]

EL NIÑO MALCRIADO: REBELLIOUSNESS AND VIOLENCE

Castro was the first of several illegitimate children born to Ángel Castro, a Spanish plantation owner, and one of his family servants. Raised in the mountainous region of Oriente province where he would later take up the struggle against Batista, Fidel grew up in a wild and

---

[4]There is, of course, the question of reliability when dealing with the accounts of former associates or family members who may have personal scores to settle or who wish to put themselves in the best light. These accounts should be checked against other sources and, where corroboration is lacking, they must be used with care.

[5]Although methodologically different, this analysis takes its inspiration from a pathfinding study by Nathan Leites, *A Study of Bolshevism*, Glencoe, Illinois: Free Press, 1963, which analyzed the "operational codes" of Lenin and other Soviet leaders. See also Vamik D. Volkan and Norman Itzkowitz, *The Immortal Ataturk—A Psychobiography*, Chicago: University of Chicago Press, 1984.

rough family environment dominated by his tough but by no means ungenerous father.[6] When Fidel was seven years old, Ángel Castro married Fidel's mother so that his son could be admitted to the Colegio La Salle in Santiago de Cuba, the first of three Catholic schools the boy attended. Fidel went from the Colegio La Salle to the Colegio Dolores in Santiago de Cuba, and then to the Belén High School in Havana, both run by the Jesuit order. Belén High School, where he excelled as an athlete, enjoyed an outstanding national reputation. He entered the University of Havana in 1945, where he earned a law degree.

The two Jesuit schools played a profound part in forging his later intellectualism, forensic skills, and values. In reminiscing about his childhood and adolescence in 1985, Fidel approvingly singled out the Jesuits for their austere, strict, and self-disciplined behavior.[7]

By all accounts, including his own, Castro was a headstrong child in frequent conflict with his father and the guardians with whom he lived while attending school. His sister described him as

> nervous and bright, capable of towering rages and violence. He had—and has retained—some of the temperamental attributes of a spoiled son. Indeed, although none of us in the family ever lacked anything, my father always gave Fidel what Fidel asked for.[8]

Ángel Castro tended to indulge his son well beyond adolescence. After graduating from Belén, Castro asked his father for a car despite the wartime shortage and resulting high cost of cars.[9] His father provided him with "a flashy V-8 Ford and a one hundred dollar monthly allowance to pay for his room in a boarding house" when he was at the University of Havana.[10] When Castro married Mirta Díaz Balart, according to Juana Castro,

---

[6]"His father, built to epic proportions of energy and bravery which Fidel would like to surpass, was one of the famous bandits of the Sierra, who murdered and robbed, drank and fornicated lavishly. By becoming a supporter of Conservative President Monocal, he legitimized his career and his seizures of property. His wife, Fidel's mother, was thrown out in favor of various mistresses." (Carleton Beals, "The New Crime of Cuba," *The Nation*, June 29, 1957, p. 567.) A critic of the Batista regime, Beals filed this report from Havana on assignment for *The Nation*. Years earlier he had interviewed Sandino in Nicaragua and was the author of several books on Latin America, including *The Crime of Cuba* (1933).

[7]*Fidel e a Religiao: Conversas com Frei Betto*.

[8]Juana Castro, "My Brother Is a Tyrant and He Must Go," *Life*, August 26, 1964, p. 25.

[9]Ibid.

[10]Pardo Llada, "Fidel: De los Jesuitas al Moncada," p. 16. Pardo Llada met Castro in 1944, became his regime's propagandist in 1959, and then was forced to leave Cuba in 1961.

> Father . . . gave them a splendid wedding and money for their honeymoon—three months of travel in the United States in a car Father bought for them. Later he gave them a house and supported them until Fidel got his law degree.[11]

But Castro was more than just a spoiled child. He was *el niño malcriado*—the misbehaving child—whose behavior was purposeful and calculating, as he himself would later admit:

> I remember I had a different attitude toward people who understood me and treated me kindly. My conduct would be entirely different, depending upon the treatment I received. There are really few people who I can remember understood me as a child.[12]

By becoming *el niño malcriado*, Fidel time and again maneuvered his parents and guardians into sending him away to boarding school, which he found far preferable to life at home. For example, "fed up" with the rules of good conduct and discipline insisted upon by his guardians, he resolved to escape:

> I deliberately disobeyed everything, I ignored all the orders, all the rules, all discipline, I spoke loudly, I said all the words I was forbidden to say, in a conscious show of rebellion, so that they would send me to boarding school. That was my first rebellion . . . I was at most 7 years old.[13]

When his father threatened to keep him out of school because of adverse reports concerning his behavior, which Fidel considered grossly "unfair," he went to his mother:

> I appealed to her and told her I wanted to stay in school and that if I wasn't sent back, I'd set fire to the house. . . . *I really threatened to set the whole place on fire if I wasn't sent back to school.* So they decided to send me back [emphasis added].[14]

Later, in the sixth grade, he again rebelled because of the "lack of understanding and bad treatment" he received in the house where he was living while going school:

---

[11]Castro, "My Brother Is a Tyrant and He Must Go," p. 25. Although he does not mention these incidents in his interview with Frei Betto, Castro himself affirmed that his father was generous toward both family members and acquaintances.

[12]Franqui, *Diary of the Cuban Revolution*, p. 8.

[13]Translated from *Fidel e a Religiao: Conversas com Frei Betto*. Describing the incident to Franqui in 1959, Castro made the same point: "I made up my mind then, and proceeded to rebel and insult them. . . . I behaved so terribly that they took me straight back to school and enrolled me as a boarder. *It was a great victory for me.* I was finally going to have the same kind of life as all the other kids." (Franqui, *Diary of the Cuban Revolution*, p. 3 (emphasis added).)

[14]Franqui, *Diary of the Cuban Revolution*, p. 5.

I had had enough of the place, and one day I stood up to the lady of the house; I told her off about the way they treated me. I told them all to go to the devil, and entered school as a boarder that very afternoon. This was the second time, or the third, fourth, fifth, I can't remember which, that I had to take it upon myself to get out of what I considered an unpleasant situation.[15]

The same pattern was repeated in the sixth grade, when at age 10 or 11, he again insisted upon returning to boarding school:

I gave notice that I would become a boarding student, or rather, I urged insistently that they make me a boarding student. *I was already an expert in those things.* I decided to create a situation in which they would have no other alternative but to send me to boarding school [emphasis added].[16]

Even in school, his behavior was often rebellious unless he had his way: "With the teacher who treated us well and brought us toys, I remember being well-behaved. But when pressure, force, or punishment was used, my conduct was entirely different."[17]

According to his brother Raúl, Castro was also in constant battle with other boys in grade school:

He succeeded in everything. In sport, in study. And every day he fought. He had a very explosive nature. He defied the most powerful and the strongest and when he was beaten he began again the next day. He never gave up.[18]

Fidel was not always graceful when he lost. After being beaten badly by Ramón Mestre, one of his schoolmates at Belén, he is reported to have sought his revenge:

Humiliated, blinded with rage, Fidel picked himself up from the floor, ran to his room—he was a boarding student—and returned with a pistol in his hand. With much effort, the Prefect, Father Larruesea, was barely able to restrain him.[19]

Years later, Castro's government sentenced Ramón Mestre to life imprisonment for counterrevolutionary activities.

Castro's childhood and adolescent behavior resembles that of juvenile delinquents who engage in violent, antisocial behavior to get their own way with parents and society. However outrageous their

---

[15]Ibid., p. 7.

[16]*Fidel e a Religiao: Conversas com Frei Betto.*

[17]Franqui, *Diary of the Cuban Revolution*, p. 2.

[18]Robert Merle, *Moncada, premier combat de Fidel Castro, 26 juillet 1953*, Paris, 1965, as quoted in Thomas, *Cuba, The Pursuit of Freedom*, p. 808.

[19]Pardo Llada, "Fidel: De los Jesuitas al Moncada," p. 14.

actions may be, such delinquents consider themselves blameless because they see themselves as victims of unfair parental or societal authority. They do not accept responsibility for their actions, but rather justify them as a legitimate reaction to an unjust world. Castro's childhood and teenage behavior became self-reinforcing because it repeatedly succeeded—in securing money from his father, in being returned to boarding school, in asserting his dominance over schoolmates.[20]

Derivative Traits: Castro as a Political Leader

From his childhood and youth, five derivative behavioral traits stand out in Castro's *modus operandi* during his later political career: the use of rebelliousness and violence to obtain high rewards, manipulative confrontation to gain concessions, extortion to generate power, punishment against those who do not submit, and rationalization of his actions on the basis of high principles. These are not the only traits that appeared in Castro's childhood and youth, but they are ones that have reappeared consistently in his political behavior.

Rebelliousness and violence to obtain high rewards. *Violent, rebellious behavior carries the risk of punishment, but, as Castro learned early on, it can also yield much higher returns than conformity. As he had done in childhood and adolescence, he later engaged in rebelliousness and political violence on both the domestic and international fronts. Such behavior became the means by which he sought maximum recognition, power, and independence.*

To advance his political ambitions as an aspiring university student leader, Castro joined one of two political-gangster "action groups," the Unión Insurreccional Revolucionaria (UIR), to break the dominance of a rival group, the Movimiento Socialista Revolucionaria (MSR), over the university. Later, after the UIR's leader was killed in a three-hour gun battle with the MSR, Castro joined with rival MSR leaders in the ill-fated Cayo Confites expedition to overthrow the dictator Trujillo in

---

[20]It can be argued that many of Castro's behavioral traits as *el niño malcriado* are socioculturally inculcated in Cuban children because Cuban parents have a propensity to tolerate certain kinds of behavior, especially by boys, that other societies might find offensive. As *el niño malcriado*, Fidel Castro can thus be considered very much a Cuban phenomenon.

However true that may be, not all Cuban children behave the way Fidel did, including his brother Raúl. Moreover, he exhibits a remarkable coldness toward his mother, father, sisters, and brothers, as evidenced not only by the accounts of former comrades such as Casuso and Franqui, but also by his own recent interview in *Fidel e a Religiao: Conversas com Frei Betto*. Such a lack of familial ties and affection is atypical of most Cubans, suggesting that Fidel was a most unusual *niño malcriado*, even by Cuban standards.

1947.[21] The following year, he tried to assume a leadership role in the "Bogotazo" or spontaneous popular upheaval that swept through much of Bogotá, where he was attending a Latin American student "anti-imperialist" conference bankrolled by the Perón government.[22] Following Batista's seizure of power, Castro launched the Moncada attack in 1953 and began waging a guerrilla campaign in 1956.

Initially, Castro's reputation as a *pistolero* and political gangster had disturbed the more moderate anti-Batista opposition, preventing him from forging links with other groups. But in time, according to a former collaborator,

> Castro's tested capacity for action and leadership stood out amid the disorganization and vacillation of all the other opposition groups. . . . Many people then, including me, saw in Castro a crude force that could be put to good use if it were properly harnessed and guided. Unfortunately . . . they think they can use the strong leader and end up by being used themselves.[23]

Indeed, not only did Castro succeed in overthrowing Batista, his stunning accomplishment gave him the charismatic authority whereby he soon assumed total power over Cuba.

The assumption of national leadership did not temper Castro's behavior. Cuba soon became the mecca and staging area for promoting a wider insurrection, first in the Caribbean and Central America, and then in the rest of the Americas. Revolutionary war and the creation of many "Vietnams" on the continent, as called for by the Havana-based Latin American Solidarity Organization (OLAS), became the means by which Castro sought to extend his influence, defeat the United States, and ensure Soviet support. Following the demise of the revolutionary movement after Che Guevara's death in 1967, Castro returned in the late 1970s to actively promoting armed struggle in Central America and elsewhere, to pursue his imperial ambitions.

Manipulative confrontation to gain concessions. *An adversary's greater strength can be overcome by manipulative forms of confrontation that exploit his vulnerabilities for maximum leverage. As in his earlier dealings with parental authority, Castro sought leverage in dealing with both superpowers through confrontational modes of behavior.*

---

[21]On Castro's university and insurrectionist activities, see Bonachea and Valdés (eds.), *Revolutionary Struggle*, pp. 19–24. The fullest and most judicious account of these activities through the guerrilla campaign is that of Thomas, *Cuba, The Pursuit of Freedom*.

[22]A detailed account of his participation in the Bogotazo is given by Castro in Franqui, *Diary of the Cuban Revolution*, pp. 9–19.

[23]Llerena, *The Unsuspected Revolution*, p. 60.

During much of the 1960s, Castro sought to gain Soviet political, economic, and security guarantees while retaining maximum independence from his new patron. As the Soviet Union's *niño malcriado*, he deviated sharply from the Soviet line on the question of armed struggle in Latin America, the use of moral over material incentives for the Cuban economy, and Cuba's claim that it was building socialism and communism simultaneously and would therefore arrive at the latter stage before the Soviets. Worse still, when relations were most strained during 1967–68 as a result of his policies, he virtually accused Moscow of forsaking its "internationalist" obligations to Cuba, Vietnam, and Latin America. He remained defiant until economic difficulties, the demise of revolutionary movements in Latin America, and Soviet cutbacks in oil deliveries finally forced him to make peace with Moscow, which he first signaled by his qualified endorsement of the Warsaw Pact invasion of Czechoslovakia in August 1968.[24]

Castro's confrontational stance toward the United States was also a means to gain leverage and recognition in dealing with Washington and Latin America. By attacking U.S. "imperialism" and promoting violent revolution in the United States' own strategic backyard, he ensures U.S. hostility. Nonetheless, he gains as the hemisphere's *niño malcriado* because he cannot be ignored by Washington, as other Latin American leaders have been. Moreover, by leading the Latin American struggle for violent, radical revolutionary change, or, more recently, by calling for a debt moratorium for the region, he acquires a measure of leverage vis-à-vis the United States that offsets the latter's preponderance of power. Castro, in short, becomes a factor that must be reckoned with by Washington in its policy toward Latin America. By the same token, he must also be reckoned with by other Latin American governments, who cannot afford to ignore his subversive activities or political stance.

Extortion to generate power. *One can deter and intimidate opponents through credible threats, even if the threatened action could also damage one's own interests. Castro demonstrated that he knew the power of extortion when he threatened to set fire to his parents' home. Such threats acquire additional credibility when he is perceived as irrational and therefore able—if not likely—to carry out a threat that results in his own loss.*

Castro's inclination to rely on political-military extortion against other states, including both superpowers, has been frequently in evi-

---

[24]See Edward Gonzalez, "Relationship with the Soviet Union," in Carmelo Mesa-Lago (ed.), *Revolutionary Change in Cuba*, Pittsburgh: University of Pittsburgh Press, 1971, pp. 81–104.

dence.²⁵ According to Carlos Franqui, for example, Castro agreed to the Soviet installation of medium- and intermediate-range missiles in 1962 not only to deter U.S. aggression, but also to threaten "the Yankees."²⁶ Despite its outcome, the crisis confirmed Castro's image as an irrational, malevolent leader bent on harming the United States, thereby enabling him to acquire a measure of power in dealing with successive U.S. administrations. This was discovered by the Carter administration when, to its consternation, Castro expelled some 2,000 convicted felons, mentally ill inmates, and other "undesirables" among the 125,000 Marielitos who fled to the United States in 1980.

Castro has also engaged in political extortion against Moscow, as demonstrated by the so-called "microfaction" affair in 1967–68. Thirty-five people, most of them former members of the old pro-Soviet Popular Socialist Party (PSP), led by former PSP Executive-Secretary Aníbal Escalante, were arrested, tried, and convicted for subversive activities; they were sentenced to prison terms ranging from 2 to 15 years. Among the charges leveled at the so-called "microfaction" was that of conspiring with Soviet and East European representatives against Castro. The Central Committee of the Communist Party of Cuba (PCC) officially disassociated the Soviet and East European governments of contacts with the conspirators, but the action taken against the "microfaction" constituted a warning to Moscow that Castro and his followers would resist Soviet interference by exposing Moscow's policies and purging former PSP members who occupied Party and government positions in the regime.

A more blatant, consistent employment of extortion is evident in Castro's policy toward individual Latin American countries. By actively promoting armed revolution and by cultivating close ties with revolutionary movements and radical groups, he in effect puts Latin American and Caribbean regimes on notice that he can validate their leftist credentials with the radical left, ease their security problems by withholding support from guerrilla movements, or intensify those problems by actively assisting revolutionary groups in their respective countries. As a consequence, some Caribbean governments, e.g., Michael Manley's in Jamaica in the 1970s, have had to play "the Cuban card" to defuse extreme-left wing opposition.²⁷ Other governments, including

---

²⁵After holding nearly 1,200 exile prisoners for ransom for twenty months following the Bay of Pigs invasion, Castro traded their freedom for $53 million worth of food and medical supplies from the United States. Although other leaders might have done the same, such a ransoming fits Castro's general pattern of using extortion tactics.

²⁶See Franqui, *Family Portrait with Fidel*, pp. 192–193.

²⁷See Anthony P. Maingot, "Cuba and the Commonwealth Caribbean: Playing the Cuban Card," in Barry B. Levine (ed.), *The New Cuban Presence in the Caribbean*, Boulder: Westview Press, 1983, pp. 22–27.

successive administrations in Mexico, have found it prudent to maintain ties with Havana to preclude Cuban-backed insurrections in their own countries. Still others have attempted to secure Havana's services in coping with guerrilla movements, as the Colombian government did to deal with the M-19.

Punishment of those who do not submit. *Those who oppose must be rendered submissive, but those who continue to defy must be punished. As in his fight with Ramón Mestre, Castro constantly lashes out against those who thwart his ambitions or refuse to submit to his domination.*

In an interview with Carlton Beals in 1957, one of Castro's political associates described Castro's behavior five years earlier:

> He was imperious and could stand no criticism. After several drinks, he would lose all self-control and turn on his closest friends, who gradually abandoned him. I think I was the one exception.[28]

Even members of his family were not spared his wrath. After assuming power, he wrote an unsigned editorial in *Revolución*, then the organ of his July 26 Movement, viciously denouncing his older brother, Ramón, who had publicly defended another newspaper in its polemics with *Revolución*.[29]

Castro's greatest intolerance was reserved for those who dared to attempt to thwart him politically. The first to go was President Manuel Urrutia, who made strong anti-Communist statements after Castro had proscribed anti-Communism. Resigning as Prime Minister on July 17, Cuba's new *caudillo* went on television, where, "in a long and extraordinary speech he destroyed the president. It was less a speech than an execution."[30] The hapless president submitted his resignation as Castro talked, after which the *líder máximo* resumed his post as Prime Minister in response to the mounting public clamor for his return to the government.[31] Three months later, Castro ordered the arrest of Major Huber Matos and his staff in Camaguey province after Matos had submitted his resignation from the army because of growing Communist infiltration of the revolution. Indicting Matos for

---

[28]Beals, "The New Crime of Cuba," p. 567.

[29]The editorial called Ramón an "unnatural brother" and leveled other personal insults at him. Soon after, Fidel informed his sister that he, not *Revolución*'s editor (Carlos Franqui), was its author. (Castro, "My Brother Is a Tyrant and He Must Go," p. 28.)

[30]Thomas, *Cuba, The Pursuit of Freedom*, p. 1232. Among other things, Castro accused Urrutia of living high off his presidential salary of $40,000 per annum, fabricating a Communist threat to provoke U.S. aggression, and obstructing government policies.

[31]Urrutia's ordeal did not end there, however. He was placed under house arrest, after which he took refuge in the Venezuelan embassy. Finally he was allowed to go into exile.

"treason" before an enormous mass rally on October 26, Castro then intervened as the star witness against Matos at his trial; the court imposed a 20-year sentence on the former guerrilla hero.

Castro himself disposed of the old Cuban Communists from the PSP when they began to challenge his leadership. He denounced Aníbal Escalante and other PSP leaders in March 1962, dispatching them into exile in Eastern Europe. When Escalante returned, he and the rest of the "microfaction" were given prison terms.

Castro has also lashed out against other heads of state who have rebuffed him or frustrated his imperial ambitions—and he continues to do so. His support for the guerrilla insurgency in Venezuela in the early 1960s, for example, may well have stemmed from President Romulo Betancourt's rejection of his request for a $300 million loan that would enable Castro to take on "the gringos."[32] Twenty years later, Havana's support for the M-19 guerrillas in Colombia may have been prompted by the fact that Colombia's candidacy for the Latin American seat in the U.N. Security Council had prevented Cuba, at the time head of the Non-Aligned Movement, from winning that seat in fall 1979.[33] More recently, Castro has conducted a personal vendetta against Peruvian President Alan García because of García's independent position on the Latin American debt crisis and his criticisms of Castro's policies.

Justification on the basis of high principles. *Whether to further one's interests or to harm an opponent, actions are always taken on the basis of high principle. Just as the world appeared unjust when he was young, so it remains for Castro in power, who rationalizes his actions as justifiable, indeed honorable, responses to the flagrant abuses and injustices committed by others.*

Castro has always had a remarkable capacity for considering himself blameless. Faced with having his weekly allowance taken away from him because of poor grades in primary school, he resorted to flagrant cheating—but according to him, it wasn't cheating because he only took steps "to protect my interests."[34] Accordingly, he is always able to assign blame to others—his ignorant parents, guardians, and teachers during childhood; later, Batista and a venal Cuban political class,

---

[32]Thomas, *Cuba, The Pursuit of Freedom*, p. 1090. Interestingly, as a 13-year-old, Castro had written President Franklin Delano Roosevelt to congratulate him on winning the 1940 elections—and to ask for $20, a request which was denied. (Thomas, p. 808.)

[33]Cuba had lined up considerable Third World support in its bid for the Security Council seat, but after an unprecedented number of ballots, neither Colombia nor Cuba had gained enough votes. The Soviet invasion of Afghanistan in late December then forced Cuba to withdraw from the race.

[34]Franqui, *Diary of the Cuban Revolution*, p. 6.

exploitative, antinational regimes in Latin America, and aggressive U.S. imperialism. Thus, he has easily rationalized his behavior on the the basis of high principle.

In recent years, Castro has offered three explicit rationales for Cuba's interventionist activities in Latin America, all of which seemingly rest on high moral principles:

- *The right to retaliate against hostile regimes.* In a 1984 interview with Tad Szulc, Castro declared that "we are disposed to fulfill our international norms and obligations [regarding nonintervention] in relations to all the countries that adjust themselves to the same principle in relation to us," thereby implying that Cuban subversion would stop if Central American and Caribbean states ceased their hostility toward Havana.[35]
- *The right to express revolutionary solidarity.* A less hostile policy does not necessarily ensure an end to Cuban subversion because, as Castro explained to Szulc, "As revolutionaries ... we feel we have the right to support politically, to support morally the revolutionaries, those who wish social change."[36]
- *The right to promote social justice.* Meeting with a British parliamentary delegation in 1982, Castro declared that Cuba was entitled to intervene in those Latin American countries where social injustice prevails—a criterion which makes most states vulnerable to Cuban "internationalist" activities.[37]

In thus giving himself *carte blanche* to engage in subversion against Latin American governments, Castro continues to justify his actions on the basis of such high principles as reciprocity among states, coreligiosity among comrades, and justice among men.

EL NIÑO MALCRIADO: THE ARTFUL DISSEMBLER

Castro has been many men to many people, including former associates who thought they knew him well. He has shown a masterful ability to dissemble and beguile, both in public and in private. He uses *deceit to mask true intentions, conceal weaknesses, exaggerate strengths, disarm opponents, and otherwise gain political advantage.*

Castro's deceitful behavior had its initial roots in his role as *el niño malcriado*. In the fifth grade, for example, he moved to prevent his

---

[35]*Los Angeles Times*, April 22, 1984.
[36]Ibid.
[37]See House of Commons, *Foreign Affairs Committee, Session 1981-1982*, October 21, 1982, Sections 203 and 204.

20-cent allowance from being cut off because of poor grades. On the pretext of having lost his notebook, he secured a new one from his teachers in which he falsified grades for his guardians to see and sign every week; he then forged their signatures in the original notebook, which he returned to his teachers. With considerable glee he recounts how he later fooled his guardians with an explanation as to why he was not awarded a prize for high marks during the school ceremony at the end of the semester:

> There I was, cool and waiting for them to say, "Fifth grade, first prize, Enrique Peralta . . . ." I started to look shocked, as if I couldn't figure it out. They began to read off the prizes for each subject and I won absolutely nothing. . . . Then I said, "Oh, darn it! . . . I know what's happened. I started very late, in December, that's why they haven't counted me in, I was three months short, so my grade totals are less than others', and that's why I'm not getting any prizes."[38]

Castro's calculating deception has reappeared throughout his political career. Writing from prison in April 1954, he advised one of his followers: "Much guile and smiles for everyone. . . . There will be ample time later to squash all the cockroaches together."[39]

In thus preparing the insurgency, a former collaborator recalls, Castro began "talking respectfully about the old parties and the old figures on Cuba's political scene with a clear sense of subordination, particularly in regard to the Ortodoxo leaders."[40] During the early phases of the guerrilla campaign he continued to portray himself as an anti-Communist, as a committed democrat and constitutionalist, and as a nationalist reformer, in order to attract the support of the Cuban middle class.[41]

Later, on a visit to the United States in April 1959, Castro publicly announced that he was taking his top economic advisers with him to enter into economic discussions with Washington; in fact, he had privately forbidden them to engage in such talks. As Franqui described Castro's encounter with then-Vice-President Nixon: "Fidel's strategy was to seem a friend to all; he would offer his hand and let the others

---

[38]Franqui, *Diary of the Cuban Revolution*, p. 7.

[39]Letter to Melba Hernández, in Luis Conte Agüero, *Cartas del Presidio*, Editorial Lex, Havana, 1959, p. 38.

[40]Llerena, *The Unsuspected Revolution*, p. 87.

[41]"As one reads Castro's succession of statements in 1956–58, the most striking thing about them is their increasing 'moderateness' and constitutionalism. . . . Significantly, Castro made very few [democratic] programmatic statements in the second half of 1958, when Batista's regime was crumbling." (Draper, *Castroism: Theory and Practice*, pp. 15–16.)

[i.e., Nixon] not shake it."[42] During the same trip, he had a three-hour private meeting with a CIA specialist on Communism, who then reportedly informed the Cuban Minister of the Treasury, Rufo López-Fresquet, that, "Castro is not only not a Communist, but he is a strong anti-Communist fighter."[43]

Cuban associates and U.S. officials were not the only ones deceived. Unlike Raúl Castro and Che Guevara, whose respective Communist affiliations and sympathies were well known, Castro's own political inclinations in 1959 remained "the greatest enigma of them all" to such close companions and radical nationalists as Carlos Franqui.[44] It was not until December 2, 1961, that Castro revealed, "I am a Marxist-Leninist and I shall be a Marxist-Leninist until I die." He admitted that he had had to hide his Marxist and "utopian socialist" orientations to minimize domestic and U.S. opposition.[45] Still, he would wait nearly another twenty-five years before disclosing the full extent to which he had already become a committed Marxist-Leninist when he was at Havana University.[46] Having thus concealed his Marxist inclinations, he not only jettisoned his democratic and "humanistic" stance after mid-1959, but also quickly radicalized the Cuban Revolution along socialist and pro-Soviet lines, to the dismay of more democratic and anti-Soviet elements in the revolutionary camp.[47]

As he did during his childhood, Castro often goes beyond dissembling to bald-faced lying. Despite the reports of Amnesty International

---

[42]Franqui, *Family Portrait with Fidel*, p. 32.

[43]Rufo López-Fresquet adds that Castro also told him: "Look, Rufo, I am letting the Communists stick their heads out so I will know who they are. And when I know them all, I'll do away with them, with one sweep of my hat." (*My Fourteen Months with Castro*, p. 110.)

[44]Franqui, *Family Portrait with Fidel*, pp. 21–24.

[45]See *Obra Revolucionaria*, December 2, 1961.

[46]This occurred in two different interviews in spring 1985. In one, Castro maintained, "I was a Marxist *before* I entered prison. Before our defeat at Moncada, which sent me to prison, I already had the deepest convictions. I had acquired them earlier, upon reading books about socialism. I was already a Utopian Communist" (emphasis in original). ("Playboy Interview," p. 68.) In his interview with Brazilian Friar Betto, Castro went into greater detail. As a result of his studies at the University, he said, "I already had a Marxist-Leninist education and a very clear revolutionary idea" by the time of the Moncada attack. But he chose not to associate himself with the Cuban Communists who "found themselves isolated because of the fence around them created by imperialism," which meant that "there was no political opportunity for them." He went on: "It was then I conceived a revolutionary strategy for placing a profound social revolution into practice by steps, by phases. Fundamentally, what I conceived was to carry it out with that great rebellious, dissatisfied mass that did not have a mature awareness about revolution but which made up the immense majority of the people. . . . It is necessary to lead that mass to revolution by phases." (Translated from *Fidel e a Religiao: Conversas com Frei Betto*.)

[47]See Franqui, *Family Portrait with Fidel*, pp. 42–62.

and other organizations of widespread human rights violations and mistreatment of political prisoners in Cuba, he insisted to his *Playboy* interviewers in March 1985 that

> the history of the Revolution contains *no* cases of physical abuse or torture! . . . no one can point to a *single* case of torture, murder or disappearance. . . . Never has a demonstration been broken up by the police in Cuba [emphasis in original].[48]

He can be equally insistent in maintaining that the Cuban people support his government because, as he informed Robert MacNeil in February 1985,

> we have always told them the truth. The people know that from the government a lie has never been told to them. And I ask you to go to the world, tour the world and go to the United States and ask if they can say what I can say, that I have never told a lie to the people.[49]

Indeed, as with his claim of high principles, he evidently is compelled to constantly proclaim his virtue.

While governments often engage in deceit, Cuban deceitfulness appears to extend to the manipulation of official statistical data. For decades, Havana has concealed the extent of the economy's poor performance or real GNP, not only through the use of Soviet-based methodological concepts, but also through the issuance of incomplete or misleading statistical series.[50] Indeed, in the captured Grenada papers, Maurice Bishop, the late Prime Minister and protege of Castro, praises Cuban expertise in "keeping two sets of records in the banks." Even Cuba's highly acclaimed gains in public health and, to a lesser extent, education have now become suspect, owing to recent evidence of statistical manipulations that portray Cuba's performance in these areas as being substantially greater than it actually was.[51] Deceit to

---

[48]"Playboy Interview," p. 67. For a summary of human rights abuses in Cuba, including the charges leveled by Amnesty International, see *Of Human Rights*, Washington, D.C.: Georgetown University, 1985. For a painful, detailed account by a former Cuban political prisoner, see Armando Valladares, *Against All Hope*, New York: Alfred A. Knopf, 1986.

[49]MacNeil/Lehrer News-Hour, February 12, 1985, Transcript #2447.

[50]See Carmelo Mesa-Lago, *The Economy of Socialist Cuba*, Pittsburgh: University of Pittsburgh Press, 1982; and Wharton Econometrics Forecasting Associates, *A Description of the Cuban Economic Analysis and Forecasting System (CEAFS) with Projections for the Cuban Economy to 1985*, Vol. II, November 1983. The World Bank's annual *World Development Report* has discontinued listing Cuba's economic performance data.

[51]See Nick Eberstadt, "Literacy and Health: The Cuban 'Model,'" *The Wall Street Journal*, December 10, 1984.

hide Cuba's vulnerabilities and inflate its accomplishments has thus become institutionalized.

RADICALISM, OPPORTUNISM, AND TACTICAL PRAGMATISM: THE *FIDELISTA* MENTALITY

The struggle against Batista was a critical formative experience for Castro that not only reinforced existing patterns of behavior, but also developed new ones that would further influence his *modus operandi* and policies after 1959. In fact, the Moncada attack and subsequent guerrilla struggle infused *fidelismo* with a far more radical content and style than orthodox Marxism-Leninism because the former was premised on human volition and action rather than on the alleged workings of historical forces.[52] More than two decades after the defeat of Batista, the guerrilla experience was resurrected with the creation of the MTT for the defense of the homeland, and with recurrent calls for militant "struggle" (*lucha*) against internal and external enemies.

Castro's war against Batista took two different forms. On July 26, 1953, he tried unsuccessfully to seize the Moncada barracks in Santiago de Cuba, the second largest military installation on the island. The assault reflected Castro's putschist inclinations, which had been evident in his earlier participation in the Cayo Confites expedition and the Bogotazo.[53] He was captured and imprisoned, but was then freed in 1955 as part of a general amnesty. After reorganizing his forces in Mexico, he resumed the struggle in Oriente province, at the southeastern end of Cuba, on December 2, 1956, having disembarked from the yacht *Granma* with 81 followers. Within two weeks, attrition and attacks from Batista's army had reduced Castro's original force to an estimated 30 men.[54] Retreating to the Sierra Maestra, Castro waged a guerrilla campaign over the next two years that ended with Batista's defeat.

Although different in form, the Moncada assault and the Sierra Maestra campaign were complementary. They both reinforced Castro's penchant for radicalism in the setting and attainment of maximum goals, and his opportunistic tendencies. The guerrilla struggle,

---

[52]On Moncada and the Sierra Maestra's contributions to Castro's mindset and policies, see Gonzalez, *Cuba Under Castro*, pp. 80–92, 106–110, and 160–163.

[53]According to Pardo Llada, Castro's putschist mentality was in evidence even earlier. As part of a four-man student delegation seeing President Grau San Martín, he allegedly proposed to his stunned companions that they throw Grau off the balcony, insisting, "This is the only opportunity we have of seizing power and we must take advantage of it." (Pardo Llada, "Fidel: De los Jesuitas al Moncada," p. 20.)

[54]According to Bonachea and Valdés (eds.), *Revolutionary Struggle*, p. 90, 21 *fidelistas* were killed and another 30 were captured by government forces.

however, also instilled a capacity for prudent calculating behavior that was new to his *modus operandi*.

The Moncada Assault Mentality

Castro's assault on the Moncada barracks was carried out by 135 men or less, with a diversionary attack in nearby Bayamo and the seizure of Radio Santiago forming part of his conspiracy. The undermanned barracks were to be seized commando-style after a night of festivities by the soldiers, the strategic objective being to spark a military and popular uprising in the rest of the island through Radio Santiago's broadcasts and appeals. However, the plan miscarried badly, as the attackers were repulsed by Batista's soldiers, the radio broadcasts were not made, and the military and civilian population did not rise in revolt. While some of the conspirators escaped, 67 were executed after being captured, and Castro and his ragged band of survivors were eventually hunted down, captured, and brought to trial.

Even in failure, however, Moncada revealed an assault mentality and two leadership tenets that would characterize many of Castro's later policies: (1) revolutionary maximalism and (2) high risk-taking.

Revolutionary maximalism. *The Moncada assault revealed Castro's propensity to stake out grandiose or breakthrough objectives for the purpose of achieving maximum economic, political, ideological, and international goals, often without regard to costs and risks.*

Among the early manifestations of Castro's maximalist tendency was his bold preemptive realignment with the Soviet Union during the post-1959 period. By rapidly radicalizing the revolution, Cuba's new leader forced a *fait accompli* upon the more cautious Soviets, who preferred to minimize their commitments to his regime:

> Fidel's strategy was to compromise the Soviet Union by rapidly deploying the structures of the Soviet state—the Communist Party and a State Security agency. But even the Soviet government was unwilling to comply. The Soviets advised patience and constantly warned us, before and after the fact, about turning Cuba into a socialist state. All Soviet emissaries, ambassadors—even Khrushchev and Mikoyan recommended calm and patience. . . . They were all shocked at the accelerated and artificial process of nationalization they saw. The more they worried, the faster Fidel went.[55]

On other fronts he called for a continent-wide revolution, launched the ruinous Revolutionary Offensive of 1968 which made Cuba the most "socialized" economy within the Soviet bloc, and set a record-breaking

---

[55]Franqui, *Family Portrait with Fidel*, p. 78.

goal of 10 million tons for the 1970 sugar harvest, which bankrupted the Cuban economy.

Since 1970, Castro's maximalist tendencies have been tempered by external, primarily Soviet-imposed constraints. As a result, he is less directly involved in economic planning, he must contend with a more bureaucratized governmental system, and he has generally had to hew closely to the Soviet line in foreign and domestic affairs. Hence, he has been less able to pursue the kind of breakthrough policies he used in the 1960s. Nevertheless, his maximalist proclivity has manifested itself in other ways in recent years—through his continuing efforts to assume leadership over the Third World and the Non-Aligned Movement and to contest imperialism in Africa, the Caribbean, and Central America. Castro thus persists in pursuing a big country's foreign policy despite Cuba's resource and technological limitations.

High risk-taking. *The Moncada assault revealed an inclination to engage in high-risk undertakings, provided there are prospects of realizing high payoffs and strategic goals.*

Defeat at Moncada did not dispel Castro's readiness to pursue high-risk gambits where the prospective gains are commensurately high. Three and a half years later, he not only sailed from Mexico in a small yacht with 81 men, but he also gave the Cuban people and Batista forewarning of his landing by announcing when he would arrive. Because he had promised to return to Cuba by 1956, he insisted on disembarking by November 30, despite the strong objections by Frank País that such a landing would be dangerously premature because Castro's underground groups in Santiago de Cuba were "unprotected, unprepared, and uncoordinated." Castro's response was to instruct Frank to "work harder to pave the way for rebellion."[56]

Castro has continued to pursue high-risk/high-gain policies since 1959, while avoiding high-risk/low-gain gambits. In defying the "Colossus of the North" and realigning Cuba with the Soviet Union, for example, he risked aggression and permanent hostility from the United States. His post-1960 realignment with Moscow, however, gained him an external guarantor for the Cuban Revolution—one that would assure his power at home and enable him to pursue his anti-imperialist ambitions abroad. In turn, his decision to permit Soviet missiles in Cuba in 1962 was motivated not only by defensive considerations, but also by his desire to gain the upper hand over Washington.

Castro's penchant for risk-taking has been further manifested by his grand strategy toward Africa, where, since the early 1960s, he has

---

[56]Bonachea and Valdés (eds.), *Revolutionary Struggle*, p. 84.

sought to forge a bloc of Cuban-led "progressive" states that would become the center of the Third World's anti-imperialist system.[57] To this end, he has repeatedly committed Cuban military units to combat roles in distant African theaters:

- In October 1963, he deployed 2,000 Cuban troops and heavy weapons to assist revolutionary Algeria in repelling a Moroccan invasion—the first use of Cuba's militarized form of "internationalism" on behalf of other revolutionary movements and regimes.[58]
- In early 1965, he secretly dispatched some 200 Cuban blacks to Tanzania, from which they entered the former Belgian Congo, seen as pivotal to the success of the anticolonial movement in Africa; they were led by Che Guevara in an unsuccessful guerrilla operation to overthrow the U.S. and Belgium-backed government of Moises Tshombe.
- In Cuba's largest overseas combat operations, Castro deployed 36,000 troops to Angola (in 1975-76) and 12,000 troops to Ethiopia (in 1977-78), gaining him elevated leadership status in Africa and the Third World, and increased Soviet support.

Although he has not deployed combat forces in the Caribbean Basin, Castro's activities there have nevertheless been aimed directly at challenging U.S. power and presence—in Grenada, Nicaragua, El Salvador, and other countries—in an effort to create new Marxist, Cuba-oriented regimes.

The Sierra Maestra Complex

The guerrilla struggle against Batista was an even more important formative experience for Castro than was Moncada. Like Moncada, it began in putschist fashion, as Castro's disembarkation was intended to spark an islandwide uprising. But he failed in this objective and had to take refuge in the Sierra Maestra, from which he waged a guerrilla war. The struggle took place over two years, under often arduous conditions.

---

[57]Castro's African strategy, which also had domestic racial roots, is exhaustively detailed by Carlos Moore, *Cuba's Race Politics: The Shaping of Castro's Africa Policy*, Center for Afro-American Studies, University of California, Los Angeles, forthcoming.

[58]Two weeks after Cuban forces had engaged in combat with Moroccan troops, Ben Bella denied that he had requested Cuban military assistance and claimed that it was Castro who had decided to add Cuban troop contingents, tanks, and other weapons to the shipments of sugar that were being delivered to Algeria. (See Claude Julien's interview of Ben Bella, *Le Monde*, November 8, 1963, p. 1.) Castro's bold action was an attempt to cement his alliance with Ben Bella's Algeria, whose collaboration with Cuba was vital to the success of Havana's African strategy.

But it succeeded spectacularly where Moncada had failed. Castro's Rebel Army (which started with a few survivors from the *Granma*) numbered no more than 2,000 guerrilla fighters when Batista fled and his 40,000-man army surrendered. The Cuban model of guerrilla war was espoused for the rest of Latin America throughout most of the 1960s by Castro, Guevara, and others, while the export of revolution became the basis of Cuban foreign policy in Latin America. At home, the guerrilla experience became part of the regime's legitimizing myth and also served as the heroic example to be emulated by Cuban workers in factories and fields.[59]

Castro's guerrilla experience produced a peculiar guerrilla mentality that further strengthened his radical and opportunistic tendencies but also included a new pragmatic dimension. The guerrilla mentality (1) stressed the importance of subjective forces, (2) embraced strategic opportunism, and (3) emphasized pragmatic adjustments over rigidity.

The importance of subjective forces. *The guerrilla victory demonstrated that subjective forces—man's will, determination, and ingenuity—can overcome objective or structural constraints.*

Castro's repeated stress and reliance on subjective forces captures the very essence of *fidelismo* as a unique form of radicalism. Unlike orthodox Marxism-Leninism, with its emphasis on political organization, preparation of the masses, and the need for favorable objective conditions, *fidelismo* assigns overriding primacy to man's ability to overcome through sheer will and determination. Castro is not to be daunted by great obstacles or adversity.

The "Sierra Maestra complex" complements the "Moncada assault mentality" by clarifying the means (human volition) by which grandiose goals can be achieved. It also reveals the egocentricity of *fidelismo*: Just as Castro succeeded in making a revolution and defying the United States, so "little Cuba" would combat imperialism by instigating revolution in the Third World during the 1960s, with the small guerrilla *foco* leading the way.

Domestically, this guerrilla mentality was evident in the literacy campaign and industrialization drive of the early 1960s, and in the 1970 sugar harvest goal. In each case, the mobilization of human resources—enthusiastic grade school students for the literacy campaign, the work force in the industrialization drive, and the military and

---

[59]Batista's downfall, it should be noted, was due not only to guerrilla war, but also to the urban resistance and conditions peculiar to pre-1959 Cuba, as other guerrilla movements subsequently learned elsewhere in Latin America. Nonetheless, Castro's triumph was the basis of his initial charismatic authority, and it infused his policies with a guerrilla radicalism. For details of the guerrilla war, see Franqui, *Diary of the Cuban Revolution*; and Bonachea and Valdés (eds.), *Revolutionary Struggle*. On the guerrilla struggle and its later impact on Castro's policies, see Gonzalez, *Cuba Under Castro*.

civilian sectors of society in the drive for 10 million tons—was the key element that was to overcome all objective obstacles. Despite the colossal failures of the latter two drives, the guerrilla mentality was not eroded, because other successes continued to confirm its perceived validity.

On the international front, for example, Castro and his followers may believe that his determination, ingenuity, and boldness have helped keep imperialism at bay, assured high levels of political, economic, and military support from Moscow, and denied Washington the option of using military force against Cuba. In this latter respect, he has organized some 1.5 million Cubans into the MTT to further strengthen Cuba's defense and deter U.S. military action. In the meantime, although his (and Guevara's) *foco* theory of guerrilla warfare failed, the triumph of the Nicaraguan Revolution vindicated Castro's stance on armed struggle, created a revolutionary ally for Cuba, and opened further prospects for revolutionary expansion into Central America.

Strategic opportunism. *The Sierra Maestra struggle revealed the need to seize the historical moment and exploit it to its fullest to gain maximum strategic advantage.*

Castro's opportunistic inclinations were already present when he joined the Cayo Confites expedition and the Bogotá riots. The Sierra Maestra campaign showed that he could make his opportunism serve strategic ends, as he consolidated his hold over the revolutionary movement by capitalizing on unexpected or fortuitous developments that eliminated potential rival revolutionary leaders from the scene and left his guerrilla movement as the only viable opposition force against Batista.[60] Following his triumph over Batista, he quickly capitalized on his charisma to overwhelm his political opposition, paving the way for his autocratic dictatorship.

Castro's strategic opportunism has imbued Cuban foreign policy with much of its dynamic, activist character: Time and again he has exploited new openings or emerging international trends and developments to shore up his regime and to further his own power and leadership ambitions. It was Castro who initiated overtures to the Soviets in the fall of 1959. Hoping to capitalize on Khrushchev's more venturesome foreign policy and thereby secure Moscow's backing for his

---

[60]Key events that Castro has exploited to his advantage were the failure of the Revolutionary Directorate to assassinate Batista in April 1957, the deaths that same year of potential rivals José Antonio Echeverría and Frank País, the failure of the April 1958 general strike, and the growing popular reaction to the repressiveness of the Batista government.

regime, he surprised the later-to-be Soviet ambassador to Cuba, Alexandr Alexeev, with his knowledge of Marxism-Leninism, and he proposed that Anastas Mikoyan visit Cuba in November following his trip to Mexico.[61]

Yet Castro also sought to maintain a measure of independence from Moscow. To gain needed allies, he worked to establish his own theaters of operation and influence in the Third World by fanning Latin American nationalism and radicalism, and by cultivating ties with the new liberationist movements and regimes in Africa in the 1960s. A decade later, he capitalized on *détente*, the U.S. policy paralysis on the heels of Vietnam and Watergate, and the new expansionist surge in Soviet foreign policy to greatly expand Cuba's military presence in Africa. Again, however, fortuitous developments enabled him to turn certain defeat into victory, this time in Angola.

Initially, the 2,000 or more Cuban military personnel Castro sent to assist the Popular Movement for the Liberation of Angola (MPLA) in September and October 1975 were overrun by invading South African forces. Hurriedly reinforcing the beleaguered Cuban troops, he succeeded only because the South Africans halted their advance. With passage in the U.S. Senate the following December of the Clark Amendment banning U.S. aid to the anti-Communist insurgents, Castro stepped up the Cuban commitment and, aided by a Soviet airlift, dispatched 36,000 Cuban combat troops to Angola to assure an MPLA victory in 1976. Beginning in November 1977, he took advantage of the Carter administration's policy of accommodation toward Cuba by embarking on a new military operation with the Soviets, eventually dispatching another 12,000 Cuban troops to Ethiopia.[62]

Castro did not act alone, however. His global outreach was abetted by the Soviet Union's more expansionist policy in the Third World, of which he took advantage for his own ends. By becoming an international paladin who actively furthered Soviet interests first in Africa and later in the Caribbean Basin, he obtained the economic backing and military resources with which to play a larger role on the world stage. Indeed, after 1975, Cuba became a privileged client of Moscow, receiving increasing levels of Soviet economic and security assistance. In terms of economic assistance alone, Soviet economic aid rose nearly

---

[61]Mikoyan was scheduled to arrive in Cuba in late November, but his visit was postponed until February 1960 because of Cuban fears that his presence would conflict with the convening of a Catholic congress in Havana. (See Alexandr Alexeev, "Cuba después del triunfo de la revolución," *America Latina* (Moscow), October 1984, pp. 62–67.)

[62]The Cuban troop figures for the Angolan and Ethiopian operation are taken from Castro's "secret speech" of December 27, 1979, to the National Assembly of People's Power. Castro's figures were 50 percent higher than Western intelligence estimates for the Angolan operation, and at least 25 percent lower for Ethiopia.

fourfold, from a cumulative total of $6.765 billion between 1961 and 1975 to $26.525 billion between 1976 and 1983.[63]

Beginning in the late 1970s, Castro also moved to exploit new openings on both the revolutionary and diplomatic fronts in Latin America. He quickly provided assistance to shore up Maurice Bishop's Marxist-Leninist regime in Grenada after the March 1979 coup. He had already capitalized on the anti-Somoza policies of other states to legitimize Cuba's involvement with the Sandinistas prior to their triumph in July 1979, thereafter quickly increasing the Cuban presence in Nicaragua to help consolidate the new regime's power. By 1980, Cuba was actively supporting the guerrilla forces in neighboring El Salvador.

Castro has seldom missed an opportunity to renew his claim to anti-imperialist leadership in Latin America, reintegrate Cuba into the broader Latin American community, and isolate the United States. In calling for Latin American solidarity with Argentina against Britain and the United States during the Falkland Islands War of 1982, he put aside his earlier condemnation of Argentina's military government. More recently, he has used the worsening Latin American debt crisis to try to assert his hemispheric leadership against the United States. For instance, at a Havana-based meeting of Latin American and Caribbean women held in June 1985, he declared that the region's debt cannot and should not be repaid, and he called for "a general strike of debtors."[64] The following month, he convened a five-day conference to promote the debt revolt, attended by roughly 1,000 politicians, writers, and academics from 17 Latin American states.

Tactical pragmatism in order to prevail. *In guerrilla war, short-term tactical adjustments must be made to survive, regroup, and attain strategic objectives over the longer term.*

The guerrilla struggle in the Sierra Maestra was a corrective to Moncada in that it forced Castro to adopt a longer time-frame and make short-term tactical accommodations to survive and then prevail over both Batista and the revolutionary movement. Since then, his ability to bide his time and retreat momentarily has helped to explain his image as a "survivor" rather than as a self-destructive zealot.

Castro's tactical pragmatism became a corollary to his guerrilla radicalism because he had to bide his time, await a favorable turn of events, and avoid large-scale frontal engagements until the Rebel Army was strong enough and government forces too demoralized to effectively resist. On the political front, he had temporarily aligned himself

---

[63]For a yearly breakdown of Soviet aid through 1983, see Edward Gonzalez, "The Cuban and Soviet Challenge in the Caribbean Basin," p. 77.

[64]See *Granma Weekly Review*, June 16, 1985, Supplement, pp. 2–8.

with the older generation of moderate, democratic opposition leaders in mid-1957 to counter the immediate challenge posed by Frank País, the less radical leader of the urban underground.[65] Soon after Castro came to power, he began to jettison the democratic coalition as he radicalized the revolution and monopolized power.

Except for the 1962 missile crisis, Castro has taken the long view and exhibited tactical flexibility in dealing with the United States, to ensure his regime's survival. Despite his "internationalist" foreign policy, he has skillfully operated below the threshold that would trigger a U.S. military response against Cuba. He thus avoided an open military confrontation with the United States over the Guantanamo Naval Base. He also moved into Africa at a time when there was less possibility of U.S. retaliation. And most recently, he has taken care to mask Cuban involvement in the Salvadoran struggle in order not to provide the Reagan administration with justification for taking armed action against Cuba.

Similarly, notwithstanding Cuban "solidarity" with Grenada, Castro's first priority was the preservation and survival of his regime, and thus the avoidance of a broader war with U.S. forces, which he made clear in a message sent to Cuban representatives on the island on October 22, 1983, just three days prior to the U.S. invasion. Because "a large-scale Yankee aggression against us" was imminent, he declared that "it is not the new Grenadian Government we must think of now, but of Cuba," and accordingly, "sending reinforcements is impossible and unthinkable."[66] As a result, the 800 or so armed Cuban construction workers on the island were left to fight the U.S. and East Caribbean forces by themselves.

Yet even while maneuvering to avoid a direct confrontation with the United States, Castro has not wavered in his determination to bring about revolution and erode U.S. influence in Latin America. He has operated in Central America in recent years as he did in the Sierra Maestra. Starting in the late 1970s, he concealed his intentions and legitimized his activities in Nicaragua by joining the democratic coalition against Somoza composed of Venezuela, Costa Rica, and Panama. In backing the Farabundo Martí National Liberation Front (FMLN) in El Salvador, he has sought to conceal Cuba's involvement in the

---

[65]This was the context surrounding the important "Sierra Maestra Manifesto" drawn up by Castro, Felipe Pazos, and Raúl Chibás. It was issued on July 12, 1957, five days after Frank País had called for a generalized armed struggle against Batista and for Castro's subordination to the July 26 Movement's collective leadership. Frank País was killed by Batista's police on July 30 after an informer had revealed his whereabouts. (See Bonachea and Valdés (eds.), *Revolutionary Struggle*, pp. 96–101.)

[66]"Statement by the Cuban Party and Government on the Imperialist Intervention in Grenada," October 25, 1983, in *Granma Weekly Review*, October 30, 1983, p. 1.

struggle and to portray it as a just war of national liberation. Although the political-military trends have now shifted against the Salvadoran insurgents, Castro appears to be taking the long view in playing for time and the emergence of more favorable revolutionary conditions.

CONSTANCY OVER CHANGE

Throughout his career, Castro has thrived on conflict and exploited confrontation to further his own personal ambitions and grand strategic objectives. Yet he has also demonstrated flexibility in adjusting to changes in domestic and international environments. Certainly over the past decade and a half he has emerged as a less radical, less rash leader than he was in the 1960s, largely because of constraints imposed by both the Soviet Union and United States. Thus, there has been no repeat of the 1962 missile crisis or the 1970 sugar harvest effort. Does this mean that Castro has become less of a radical revolutionary with a hubris-nemesis complex, and more of a pragmatic statesman? The evidence suggests this is not the case, despite his greater pragmatism at home and abroad.

Continuity in Strategic Objectives

Since coming to power, Castro has sought to ensure a set of minimum interests in his foreign policy, while also pursuing larger maximum objectives. His minimum interests have been to (1) enhance his political power base, (2) assure his regime's security, (3) maintain internal autonomy as a Soviet client-state, and (4) obtain sufficient levels of Soviet economic support for development. To a large extent, these minimum goals correspond to and can be assured by the more pragmatic dimension of Castro's behavior. He has taken care to avoid a direct confrontation with the United States in order to ensure his regime's survival. Similarly, he yielded during the 1970s to pressures from Moscow to institutionalize his regime, and he adopted economic policies along the lines of the Soviet model in order to guarantee continued high levels of economic support.

In addition to his minimum interests, Castro has also pursued a set of maximum goals that impart an offensive aspect to his international behavior and that are consistent with his hubris-nemesis complex. These are:

- To lead the Latin American and Third World struggle against "imperialism," to erode the global power and presence of the United States.

- To extend Cuba's influence and presence in Africa and Latin America through an active diplomatic, political, technical, and military-security presence.
- To promote the rise of radical-left or Marxist-Leninist regimes aligned with Cuba in the Caribbean Basin by means of armed struggle, coups, or other revolutionary means.
- To increase Cuba's power potential as a regional and global actor through the infusion of higher levels of Soviet economic and military support.
- To expand Cuba's freedom of action abroad through increased leverage over the Soviet Union.

To be sure, domestic and especially international conditions have not always permitted Castro to pursue these objectives. As evidenced by his policies over the past decade, however, they remain as strong today as they were in the 1960s—perhaps even stronger because of increases in Soviet global capabilities and new targets of revolutionary opportunity. Moreover, as power-maximizing goals, they require corresponding forms of maximalist rather than pragmatic behavior.

Continuity in Strategic Behavior

The constancy of Castro's maximum goals allows for little change in his behavior except at the tactical level. On both the domestic and international fronts, Castro's *modus operandi* continues to fit the following syllogism:

- Under certain conditions, pragmatism may be required to buy time, conserve power, and protect realized gains.
- Rebelliousness, radicalism, and strategic opportunism, however, are the only means by which maximum objectives can be attained.
- Pragmatism is thus a short-term tactic that must not stand in the way of resuming the revolutionary offensive when the opportunity reemerges.[67]

---

[67]Manuel Sánchez Pérez arrives at essentially the same conclusions. He says that Castro is committed to "military adventures" abroad because that is the only means he has of effectively projecting his own and Cuba's image onto the international stage. Havana's off-and-on overtures toward the United States, Sánchez says, enable Castro to manipulate the U.S.-Cuban relationship to his own domestic political advantage when he chooses to blame Washington for "aggression" or an "unjustified act" toward Cuba. "I think," Sánchez adds, "that there is no serious intention [by Castro] to reconcile himself with the United States." (Radio interview with Manuel Sánchez Pérez, Madrid, December 1985.)

The syllogism explains why Castro does not follow a pragmatic course for long, and why Cuba becomes "a ready and willing abettor and supporter of assorted discontent and disgruntlements throughout the Third World, always on the lookout for potential rewards for its moves."[68]

A more pragmatic Castro appeared to emerge on two occasions during the middle to late 1970s, once during the Ford administration, and then later, in the Carter administration. Cuba began to move toward some kind of normalization with Washington, culminating in the establishment of mutual interests sections in each other's capitals in September 1977. In each instance, the Cuban leader appeared to be responding not only to more accommodative signals from Washington, but also to pressures from the more moderate technocratic groups within his regime who saw economic ties with the United States as highly beneficial. Throughout most of 1977, in fact, there were good prospects that a normalization of commercial relations would occur, as Cuba's minister of foreign trade and other officials visited the United States, while U.S. business delegations were hosted by Havana.

In each instance, however, Castro's pragmatic moves toward normalization were halted when he abruptly dispatched Cuban combat troops to Angola and Ethiopia. Supported by hardline *fidelista* and *raúlista* civilian and military elites, Castro's more rebellious, radical, and opportunistic tendencies reasserted themselves as the means for advancing his personal and strategic goals. On the one hand, he strengthened his position within the regime and curbed the influence of the technocrats; his African operations strengthened his ties with the Soviets, while interrupting a normalization process that could have heightened the influence of moderate elements and undermined his authority. On the other hand, the African incursions bolstered his claim to Third World leadership and enabled him, as a paladin advancing Soviet global interests, to command much higher levels of economic and security assistance from the USSR.[69] As in the past, therefore, Castro found that pragmatism could not advance his power and leadership ambitions, and he opted for an expansionist, highly activist "internationalist" posture that could.

---

[68] Antonio Jorge, "How Exportable Is the Cuban Model?" in Levine (ed.), *The New Cuban Presence in the Caribbean*, p. 229.

[69] See Edward Gonzalez, "Institutionalization, Political Elites, and Foreign Policies," in Cole Blasier and Carmelo Mesa-Lago (eds.), *Cuba in the World*, Pittsburgh: University of Pittsburgh Press, 1979, pp. 3–37; and Edward Gonzalez, "Cuba: The Impasse," in Robert Wesson (ed.), *U.S. Influence in Latin America in the 1980s*, New York: Praeger Publishers and Hoover Institution Press, 1982, pp. 198–216.

For the foreseeable future, there is little reason to expect that Castro will alter either his basic goals or his behavior, other than for tactical considerations:

- Nearing 60 years of age, he is likely to become more rather than less rigid in his goals and political behavior.[70] This is evident in his fulminations against the reemergence of "shameful" capitalist practices in Cuba in his April 19, 1986, speech on the 25th anniversary of the Bay of Pigs (Playa Girón), and by his abolition of the peasant free market a month later.
- As he has found throughout his career, changes in the international and domestic environments can work to Castro's advantage as well as against him. Hence, he is far more likely to play for time than to compromise his objectives when faced with adversity, even though his time will grow shorter as the years pass by.[71]
- He is unlikely to alter his basic behavior primarily because it has in fact worked quite effectively over the past several decades toward the realization of his personal aspirations and his grand strategic objectives.

Indeed, precisely because his hubris-nemesis complex and *modus operandi* have served him so well in the domestic and international arenas, he has not been obliged to alter his belief system or fundamentally change his behavior to reduce "cognitive dissonance" in dealing with "objective reality."[72]

Now that the Third Party Congress of February 1986 is behind him, Castro must look to the future. He faces new types of challenges—strains and problems within Cuba, Soviet demands for improvements

---

[70]There is uncertainty as to whether Castro was born on August 13, 1926 or 1927. Two different writers who once had extensive contacts in Cuba maintain that the correct year is 1927, because Castro's parents misled school authorities in order to enroll him in primary school when he was still underage. (See Lionel Martin, *The Early Fidel*, Secaucus, New Jersey: Lyle Stuart, Inc., 1978, p. 23; and Maurice Halperin, *The Taming of Fidel Castro*, Berkeley: University of California Press, 1981, p. 1.) Official Cuban sources, including Castro himself in his 1985 interview with Friar Betto, however, cite 1926 as his birth year.

[71]Indeed, with age he may become less prudent and more inclined to act radically to achieve a major breakthrough precisely because his margin of time is diminishing.

[72]On the contrary, where the domestic or international situations have not met his expectations, Castro has found a ready reason (or culprit) behind the undesired development; or he has sought to change the world through maximalist forms of behavior; or he has accommodated to the world through short-term tactical adjustments in behavior without, however, abandoning his long-term strategic vision. As indicated in the next section, he may even avoid dealing with domestic issues that might challenge his belief system by shifting his attention to the international stage.

in Cuba's economic performance, adverse shifts in the international correlation of forces, and an unyielding if not counterattacking posture by the Reagan administration, among others—that will tax his leadership, perhaps more than ever before. We turn next to an assessment of Castro's current reading of his domestic and international situations.

IV. CASTRO AND CUBA

Castro's unique mindset and enduring *modus operandi* provide only a partial guide to what he may do next. What he chooses to do depends ultimately on how he assesses specific developments and trends, opportunities and risks in the world around him. For the past twenty-seven years, he has demonstrated an uncanny ability to analyze his domestic and international environments accurately enough to sustain his domestic rule and international influence. He has made errors, at times acting rashly and irrationally, but his overall success rate is phenomenal.

The method by which Castro assesses Cuba's domestic conditions and the international context must, for the outside observer, be largely a matter of conjecture and inference. However, we have used principles and priorities that Castro has described in his own statements, piecing together recent developments and trends, to identify elements of his likely world view, particularly regarding the challenges and opportunities he may face at home and abroad.

On the domestic front, Castro's personal power appears to be secure and to rest on a strong state apparatus. But he confronts political and economic problems that are more complex, less tractable, and less susceptible to major breakthroughs than ever before:

- He must assure the support of the coalition of elites and institutions that comprise his regime—but the coalition's growing complexity and Soviet ties make it difficult to manage while preserving *fidelista* dominance.
- He must limit the military's political and institutional strengths at home—yet he must also accommodate the professional interests of the armed forces and assure their proficiency in carrying out their internal and overseas missions.
- He must continue to militarize society in order to revive the waning revolutionary spirit of the people—but this is at cross purposes with the new economic priorities he has announced for Cuba.
- He must heed Soviet pressures to rationalize administration and improve economic performance—yet steps in this direction could strengthen the hand of Soviet-backed technocrats who want to limit his decisionmaking role.

- The economy shows little prospect of improvement, internal affairs are more a matter of administration than leadership, and daily governance needs to be entrusted to subordinates—but Castro must take care to devise a formula that will leave his power and authority intact.

These problems are probably manageable over the near to medium term. Still, Castro must ensure that they do not cause him to turn inward or constrain his freedom of action abroad. He would prefer to look outward because that is where he may be most able to score new triumphs that will redound to his own domestic advantage.

ATTENTION TO DOMESTIC AND INTERNATIONAL LINKAGES

Castro thinks systemically, globally; he is constantly attentive to the interplay between domestic and international developments. For example, his struggle against the United States, as an expression of Cuban nationalism, has repeatedly served to mobilize the populace behind his regime, as with the recent buildup of the MTT and the 1984 campaign of militarization and patriotism in "the war of all the people." In addition, he has used the estimated 65,000 Cuban military and civilian "internationalists" currently serving in Africa, the Middle East, and Nicaragua not only to advance his foreign policy ambitions,[1] but also to dissipate domestic underemployment and to symbolize the emergence of the "new man" in Cuba.[2]

He has also used foreign policy to shift internal elite balances in his favor. His dispatch of Cuban combat troops to Angola in late summer and fall 1975, for example, served to strengthen his already strong position and that of hardline *fidelista* and *raúlista* elites. It also arrested the further ascendancy of the more moderate, technocratic elements in his regime whose fortunes had steadily been on the rise since 1970.

---

[1]According to U.S. State Department figures, 44,000 Cuban military personnel serve abroad; 30,000 combat troops and 5,000 advisers are in Angola alone. An additional 21,000 civilian advisers, technicians, and aid personnel are also stationed abroad. (*Los Angeles Times*, December 6, 1985, p. 16.)

[2]As conceived by Che Guevara in *Man and Socialism in Cuba*, the "new man" was a self-directed as well as selfless individual who would willingly volunteer to serve on behalf of an international cause, as Che himself did. In contrast, the army reservists or civilian medical, technical, and teaching personnel who comprise Cuba's "internationalists" may be obliged to serve abroad either because they have no alternative (as in the case of reservists who face disciplinary action if they disobey orders) or because their future professional careers could be damaged if they do not volunteer. Until recently, those who volunteered could expect favored treatment after they returned to Cuba.

At the same time, Castro has developed Cuban "internationalism" in a way that gives even Cuba's domestic ministries and agencies vested institutional interest in having an active foreign policy.³ They benefit organizationally from enhanced prestige, expanded roles, enlarged budgets, and, in the case of the FAR, new weapon inventories. The supporting cast behind Cuban foreign policy thus includes not only individual but also institutional actors: the Ministries of the FAR and Interior, the Party's America Department, and those civilian ministries tasked with overseas missions in public health, education, and construction.⁴

Finally, Castro has pursued triumphs abroad to compensate for, or distract from, recurrent problems at home. This occurred repeatedly during the 1960s, as he sought to promote armed revolution in Latin America while the Cuban economy steadily deteriorated. The 1980 Mariel exodus and other recent signs of domestic discontent may also have helped motivate him to increase Cuba's support for revolution in Central America in the post-1980 period.

There is but one period when the deterioration in Cuba's internal situation and the weakening of his authority forced Castro to turn inward and temporarily abandon his maximalist foreign policy posture. This happened immediately before and after the disastrous sugar harvest of 1970.⁵

What are Castro's current domestic concerns? Is the present state of Cuban political and economic affairs likely to inhibit his international behavior in the foreseeable future as it did a decade and a half ago?

FORTRESS CUBA AND ITS VULNERABILITIES

Having convened the Third Party Congress in February 1986, Castro's greatest strengths remain in the areas of personal power and

---

³Cuba's activist foreign policy has also been institutionalized through its 1976 Constitution and successive Communist Party programs which reaffirm Cuba's right to support revolutionary movements throughout the world. This commitment to internationalism was again expressed in the draft platform presented at the Third Party Congress in February 1986.

⁴See Gonzalez, "Institutionalization, Political Elites, and Foreign Policies," pp. 3–36. See also Edward Gonzalez, "Complexities of Cuban Foreign Policy," *Problems of Communism*, November-December 1977, pp. 1–15.

⁵It is, of course, difficult to assign precise causality to Castro's behavior where both internal and external factors are at play. Thus, the lack of international opportunities after 1967 and the increasing Soviet pressure on Havana were certainly principal factors in Cuba's adoption of a more moderate, diplomatic posture until 1975, as were the political and economic effects of the 1970 harvest failure.

state security. However, political and especially economic vulnerabilities persist and must be addressed. Indeed, unsettled questions over how best to resolve some of these problems, together with the need to synchronize the PCC meeting with the Twenty-Seventh Congress of the CPSU that was also held in February, may explain the sudden rescheduling in July 1985 of the Third Party Congress from December to February. Yet the kinds of problems Castro and his regime now face are not likely to be resolved in the short term, as evidenced by the tone of that Party Congress.

Secure personal power. After twenty-seven years securely in power, Castro is still not likely to be openly challenged from within the regime. With the "institutionalization of the revolution" in the 1970s, his *de facto caudillistic* powers became formalized in his multiple roles as Party First Secretary, President of both the Council of State and Council of Ministers, and Commander-in-Chief of the FAR. At the Third Party Congress, he was reinstalled as PCC First Secretary to the acclaim of the nearly 1,800 delegates in attendance.

Castro surrounds himself with trusted subordinates at the highest levels of the Party, government, and state, none of whom enjoy mass support or command independent sources of power—except perhaps his brother. Raúl Castro may be the exception not only because he is second to Fidel in the Party, government, and state and is Fidel's designated heir, but also because he commands the military as Army General and Minister of the FAR and has his own *raúlista* following.[6] Despite his personal dominance and the backing of his brother, Fidel Castro cannot be overconfident concerning his own power because, as discussed below, the power elite is becoming increasingly complex.

A powerful state apparatus. Castro must feel that his regime is secure. The state he has built rests on (1) a powerful military establishment, the FAR, which has over 160,000 officers and enlisted personnel on active duty plus 135,000 ready-reserve army personnel; (2) an effective internal security apparatus within the Ministry of Interior; (3) a Party organization of over 500,000 full and candidate members; and (4) a network of mass organizations that envelops much of the Cuban citizenry. The cadres staffing these organizations have a material and ideological stake in the present system and therefore are not likely to plot its demise.

---

[6]Initially, the *raúlistas* served under Raúl Castro when he established the Second Front in 1958 during the guerrilla struggle. Many later remained in the armed forces as professional military officers. The post-1959 generation of military officers, which has received better technical training, appears to be increasingly critical of the older generation of *raúlista* and *fidelista* guerrilla veterans who continue to hold top positions within the military command structure.

This machinery of state power has recently been augmented by the 1.5 million men and women now enrolled in the MTT. The militia ostensibly serves as a rear guard in the event of U.S. aggression, but it also heightens internal political controls through the militarization of society, acts as a counterweight to the FAR, and releases the latter for combat missions abroad.

Despite the solidity of his power, Castro faces political uncertainties and economic problems that are likely to intensify in the years ahead. His major concerns appear to be (1) balancing elite groupings, (2) controlling the military, (3) reviving the revolutionary commitment of the masses, and (4) coping with economic troubles.

MAINTAINING ELITE BALANCES AND SUPPORT

For all his power, Castro cannot rule alone. He must maintain a political balance among elites and institutional forces that will ensure his power and support for his policies. He also must secure needed expertise to run the state and fulfill Cuba's international roles, which means that he must increasingly reward performance as well as political loyalty.[7] Thus, even as he must assure the continued dominance of the *fidelista* and *raúlista* elites and accommodate his powerful military establishment, he must also leave room for other elite elements to ascend, including more technocratic elements whom he needs to administer the economy.

In recent years, the Cuban elite has become broader, more difficult to manage and control, and more institutionalized, with well-defined organizational interests emerging in both the civilian and military sectors. These changes reflect the inclusion and expanding roles of a younger generation of aspirant leaders who manage the bureaucracy or, as in the case of the FAR, have participated in the African campaigns. Among these newer civilian and military officials are blacks and mulattoes who have yet to gain a share of political power that even begins to approximate their share of the island's population or that reflects their disproportionate participation in the Angolan and Ethiopian military operations. Many of the younger aspirants also have bureaucratic and professional ties to Moscow that can buttress their position within the regime.

---

[7]According to one Havana-based report, "Fidel Castro can no longer carry out his will, but nothing can happen against his will." (*Die Zeit*, February 21, 1986, p. 6.)

Managing the Generational and Racial Problems

As the years go by, Castro faces a new generation of aspiring elites who are younger, better trained, and less tied to him by bonds of personal loyalty and common revolutionary experience than are the veterans of the anti-Batista struggle. Because of their impotence in the face of the opposition of Castro and his followers to liberalizing reforms, these upper-level officials are deeply pessimistic concerning Cuba's economic future.[8] They see their further ascendancy blocked by the continuance in power of Castro's generation of leaders—those born between 1925 and 1934.

This blockage is most pronounced in the Party, because its leading organs, especially the Political Bureau, are the bastions of political power. Heavily dominated by the two Castro brothers and their followers, there has been little leadership rotation in the highest Party organs until the Third Party Congress. Nine of the eleven original members of the PCC Political Bureau and Secretariat were reappointed in 1980, with the remaining two either dead (Dorticós) or demoted (Chomón). Rather than eliminating former revolutionary comrades, Castro has preferred to increase the size of the Party's leading organs, while making sure that his *fidelista* and *raúlista* followers enjoyed an overwhelming majority of the membership. In 1980, he thus enlarged the original membership of the Political Bureau from 8 to 16 regular members, and he created a new list of 12 (nonvoting) alternates; he enlarged the Secretariat from 3 to 9 members; and he expanded the Central Committee from 100 to 146 regular members plus 77 new (nonvoting) alternates in 1980.

The new Party leadership unveiled at the Third Party Congress shows marked deviations from this past pattern, including:

- The departure of three former comrades-in-arms—Ramiro Valdés, Guillermo García, and Sergio del Valle—from the Political Bureau, evidently for reasons of poor performance and possibly policy differences (Valdés), marking the first time these

---

[8]According to Manuel Sánchez Pérez, the Cuban Vice Minister who defected in Spain in December 1985, "[W]e have tried to introduce reforms, without modifying the basic scheme of socialist production, but not even these scarcely liberalized reforms have succeeded because of ideological problems . . . [at] the highest levels of leadership in Cuba." As a result, there is "pessimism and skepticism and doubt" among the 250 or so officials at the vice-ministerial and ministerial levels concerning Cuba's economic future: "There is little hope of being able to improve the situation . . . not even in the projections for the year 2000 are there solid prospects of being able to transform the Cuban economy in a way that would convert it into a genuinely efficient and developed economy." (Radio interview with Manuel Sánchez Pérez, Madrid, December 1985.)

veteran *fidelistas* have been missing from the Political Bureau since its creation in 1965.
- The reduction in size of the Political Bureau from 16 (in 1980) to 14 regular members and its alternate list from 12 to 10, with technocrats now being conspicuous by their absence (the Secretariat remains at 9 members).
- The retention of a 225-member Central Committee (146 regular members and 79 alternates) as old regular and alternate members were dropped to make way for new ones, with 50 percent of the regular membership being replaced.
- The accommodation of younger aspirant elites in the Central Committee; the 28- to 45-year-old age group accounts for over 49 percent of the new body's combined (regular and alternate) membership, whereas Castro's generation had accounted for over 56 percent of the total membership in 1980.[9]

Although the two Castro brothers and their followers continue to dominate the Political Bureau, these changes in the Central Committee suggest that Castro may well have conceded to generational pressures within the Party. The removal of some of the old guard from high government and now high Party posts also suggests a greater awareness that performance—but not necessarily technical competence—as well as political loyalty is essential for effective governance. In both respects, Castro appears to be bowing to Soviet pressures to institute Gorbachev-type leadership changes.

Because of the regime's essentially white, middle-class Hispanic origins, the racial issue has remained a highly sensitive one for Cuba, where Afro-Cubans have been estimated to comprise 50 percent or more of the island's population.[10] Blacks and mulattoes were represented by only one black, Juan Almeida, in the Political Bureau

---

[9]When other age categories are used, however, the 1986 Central Committee actually shows an aging membership. Of the regular (voting) members, 76.7 percent of the 1986 body are 46 years or older, compared with 63.7 for the 1980 membership. When the combined membership is tallied, 50.6 percent are 46 years or older in the 1986 Central Committee compared with 49.3 percent for the regular and alternate membership in 1980. (See Office of Research and Policy, Radio Martí, *Cuba Quarterly Situation Report*, ORP/AN/QSR/Q, Vol. II, No. 1, May 14, 1986, App. III.)

[10]Although the regime did not release the 1970 census figures on race, the 1981 official census showed a slight decrease in the island's white population compared with the 1953 census: white = 66 percent (72.8 percent in 1953); mulatto = 21.9 percent (14.5 percent in 1953); and black = 12.0 percent (12.4 percent in 1953). But some ethnologists and demographers believe the 1981 figures understate the black and mulatto distribution because of the largely white exodus from the island after 1959 and the rapid growth of the Afro-Cuban population since then. Accordingly, they estimate the Afro-Cubans to comprise 50 or perhaps even as much as 66 percent of the population, with the variance stemming largely from the subjective problem of identifying the mulatto population.

between 1965 and 1975. Almeida was joined by Blas Roca in the 1975 and 1980 Political Bureau, while Miguel José Cano Blanco was added as an alternate (nonvoting) member in 1980 but was dropped in 1986. In 1986, the aging Blas Roca was also dropped and replaced by Esteban Lazo Hernández as full member, which left the number of Afro-Cubans (2) unchanged in the new 14-member Political Bureau.

However, the move toward affirmative action was more pronounced in the 1986 Central Committee, where nearly 34 percent of the *new* regular and alternate members are black or mulatto. Altogether, over 28 percent of the members of the 1986 Central Committee consider themselves to be of Afro-Cuban origin.[11] Although the proportion is still modest, the new emphasis on affirmative action suggests that the regime recognizes that it can no longer practice racial discrimination, particularly as Afro-Cubans serving in Africa show signs of having regained a new sense of ethnicity. Thus, in his main report to the Third Party Congress, Castro announced, "In order for the Party's leadership to duly reflect the ethnic composition of our people, it must include those compatriots of proven revolutionary merit and talents *who in the past have been discriminated against because of their skin color* (emphasis added)."[12]

Notwithstanding the changes made at the Third Party Congress, the composition of the new Political Bureau still shows Castro's continued personal dominance. However, it is Raúl and his following who have been strengthened the most:

- The three ousted *fidelista* veterans were replaced by two *raúlistas*: Division General Abelardo Colomé (a First Vice Minister in the Ministry of the FAR (MINFAR) who earlier distinguished himself in Angola and Ethiopia) and Vilma Espín (Raúl's ex-wife and the head of the Federation of Cuban Women).

---

[11]As with the age issue, it is possible that the regime has overstated the proportion of blacks and mulattoes in the new Central Committee. Radio Martí performed an analysis based on color photographs and the statements of three judges and recent high-level defectors from the regime, which showed that blacks and mulattos make up only 22 percent of the regular membership, compared with 34.5 percent in 1980; and that they make up 32.9 percent of the alternate membership and 24.9 percent of the total regular and alternate members (no comparative data are given for 1980). (*Quarterly Situation Report*, App. II.)

[12]*Granma Weekly Review*, February 16, 1986, p. 15. The regime also made affirmative-action-type moves regarding women: In addition to Vilma Espín's elevation to the Political Bureau, two women were added as alternates to that body; the number of women in the Central Committee also increased to 41, nearly 19 percent of the regular and alternate membership.

- Two new additions—Roberto Veiga, head of the Confederation of Cuban Workers, and Esteban Lazo Hernández, First Party Secretary of Matanzas province—are political appointees who are likely to remain tied closely to the Castro brothers.
- With the non-reappointment of aging ex-PSP leader Blas Roca and the earlier demise of another PSP leader (Arnaldo Milian), Carlos Rafael Rodríguez is the lone survivor from the PSP group (the 1980 membership, in contrast, had three ex-PSP leaders).
- With the non-reappointment of Humberto Pérez as an alternate member in the Political Bureau, technocrats and other economic specialists have virtually no representation in that body, save for the presence of Carlos Rafael Rodríguez.

In sum, there is now an even greater concentration of *fidelistas* (6) and especially *raúlistas* (5) in the new Political Bureau, thereby further entrenching the Castro dynasty.[13]

In recent years, the outlook for upward mobility by non-*fidelista* and non-*raúlista* elites has been better in the higher echelons of the government, where the "demands of complexity and leadership have opened up significant avenues of power for a new type of Cuban government leader."[14] The reshuffling of government positions that took place during the last half of 1985, and which probably will continue into 1986, may open up further opportunities for advancement. Still, the government remains subordinate to the Party, which continues to be dominated by the *fidelista-raúlista* oligarchy. Real political power may thus remain elusive for the "children of the revolution" well into the 1990s, providing a major source of friction within the regime and a growing problem for Castro in the years ahead.

---

[13]The 16-member Political Bureau in 1980 had 10 *fidelistas*, of whom 6 were guerrilla veterans, 3 were *raúlistas*, and 3 were ex-PSP members. Besides Fidel and Raúl, the make-up and pre-1959 affiliations of the 1986 membership are Juan Almeida (*fidelista*, guerrilla); Julio Camacho (*fidelista*, urban resistance); Osmani Cienfuegos (*fidelista*, urban resistance); Abelardo Colomé (*raúlista*, guerrilla); Vilma Espín (*raúlista*, guerrilla); Armando Hart (*fidelista*, urban resistance); Esteban Lazo Hernández (none); José Ramón Machado Ventura (*raúlista*, guerrilla); Pedro Miret (*fidelista*, guerrilla); Jorge Risquet (*raúlista*, guerrilla); Carlos Rafael Rodríguez (PSP); and Roberto Veiga (unknown). The new members are Colomé, Espín, Hernández, and Veiga.

[14]Jorge I. Domínguez, "Succession in Cuba: Institutional Strengths and Weaknesses," in The Cuban Studies Project, *Problems of Political Succession in Cuba*, Institute of Interamerican Studies, Graduate School of International Studies, University of Miami, 1985, p. 33. The expansion of the Council of Ministers to 11 Vice-President positions, Domínguez notes, facilitated the inclusion of some technocrats, while there was even more diffusion of formal power in the appointment of the 22 ordinary Ministers of Government, of whom only 12 belonged to the Central Committee as regular or alternate members.

Curbing Soviet-Linked Circles

During 1985 and into early 1986, the regime underwent a major shake-up as more than a half dozen high-ranking officials—including three prominent *fidelistas*—were removed from their positions in the Party or Council of Ministers prior to the Party Congress. The dismissals of Antonio Pérez Herrero and Humberto Pérez in January and July 1985, respectively, involved alleged deficiencies in performance. Although the exact details remain obscured, Pérez Herrero, as PCC Secretary for Ideology, evidently was blamed for failure to ensure that the military officers dispatched to Grenada had been properly inculcated with revolutionary consciousness—they disobeyed Castro's order to fight to the death when the American invasion began.[15] As a Vice-President of the Council of Ministers and head of the Central Planning Board (JUCEPLAN), Humberto Pérez was faulted for budgetary, planning, and other problems in the economy.

There may also have been broader considerations that made these two officials particularly vulnerable to dismissal by Castro. Their dismissals had three elements in common:

- They came at a time when Castro's leadership was vulnerable to criticism because of the setback in Grenada, an about-face in his posture toward Washington, and the mounting pressure from Moscow to improve economic administration and production.
- They involved officials who may not only have had policy differences with Castro, but also ties to the CPSU hierarchy and the Soviet administrative apparatus, both of which were critical of Castro's policies.
- They served to reaffirm Castro's personal power over the regime.

Each dismissal, however, had its specific causes.

As a former member of the old PSP youth movement and Raúl Castro's staff during the guerrilla struggle, Pérez Herrero was known as

---

[15]In addition to Pérez Herrero, his subordinate, Orlando Fundora, who headed the Central Committee's Revolutionary Orientation Department, was removed. Pérez Herrero was not dropped from the Central Committee, according to *Granma*, because his "shortcomings and repeated errors" were "not errors of principle." (*Granma Weekly Review*, February 10, 1985, p. 3.) Grenada may also have caused Division General Sixto Batista, a Vice Minister in MINFAR, and Chief of the Central Political Directorate of the FAR, to be transferred to the Military Department of the Central Committee in 1984. The fact that he was appointed to the new nine-member Party Secretariat in February 1986, however, indicates that either he was not blamed for the Grenadian affair or he was shielded by his status as a former guerrilla veteran.

an ideological hardliner. He may thus have opposed Castro's migration agreement with the Reagan administration in December 1984, as well as his opening to the Catholic Church the following month. Both of these moves augured an ideological softening of the revolution, reminiscent of the process that precipitated the explosive unrest that led to the Mariel exodus in 1980.[16] In any event, Castro reacted swiftly to what appears to have been opposition from Pérez Herrero: He convened a special plenum of the PCC Central Committee which resulted in not only the removal of the Secretary for Ideology, but also the Committee's full endorsement of Castro's policies and praise for his "tireless, creative work."[17]

Trained in Moscow, Humberto Pérez headed the technocrats charged with the task of implementing the Soviet-based System of Economic Management and Planning (SDPE). Both JUCEPLAN and SDPE had met with mixed results—and with criticisms from Castro. In December 1984, he rejected JUCEPLAN's central plan for 1985 and appointed a long-time political follower, Osmani Cienfuegos, to head a high-level ad hoc group to revise it. In a public self-criticism of the deficiencies of JUCEPLAN and SDPE, Humberto Pérez later noted that errors in both had been rectified in light of "what Comrade Fidel has rightly called a 'revolution in the economy' since the end of last year."[18] But his *mea culpa* did not save him from being replaced at JUCEPLAN by a non-economist, José López Moreno, the Minister of Construction, in July.[19]

Humberto Pérez may also have run afoul of Castro because of more fundamental issues having to do with Moscow's involvement in Cuba's domestic policies through Soviet-backed Cuban officials; whether estab-

---

[16]Starting in late 1978, the Castro regime allowed over 120,000 Cuban exiles from the United States to return to the island on brief visits, in an apparent effort to split the exile community and gain needed dollars for Cuba's hard-pressed economy. Their return had a destabilizing effect, however. The exiles contradicted the regime's propaganda concerning conditions in the United States, while vividly demonstrating how much better off they were materially than the Cubans who had remained on the island. Popular discontent exploded in April 1980, with the occupation of the Peruvian embassy by 10,000 Cubans seeking asylum, leading to the exodus of some 125,000 Cubans to the United States in the boatlift across the Florida straits between May and September 1980. Had Castro not closed the escape valve, several hundred thousand more Cubans would probably have fled the island.

[17]*Granma Weekly Review*, February 10, 1985, p. 3. Humberto Pérez did not retain his position as an alternate member of the PCC Political Bureau, but continued on as a member of the 1986 Central Committee.

[18]See the interview of Humberto Pérez by Rafael Calcines in *Bohemia*, March 19, 1985, pp. 8–17.

[19]In his Report to the Third Party Congress, Castro criticized the budget for having been "a passive, nonregulating tool" that encouraged spending and inadequate social consumption." (*FBIS*, February 7, 1986, p. Q18.)

lished institutional mechanisms and processes can function in a context where *caudillismo* has tended to prevail; and whether economists and technocrats can oppose the *líder máximo's* policies and style of governance. The Humberto Pérez affair is thus symptomatic of the tension between Castro and his Soviet-backed economists and technocrats.[20]

Whatever the immediate causes for the two dismissals, Castro may have sought to remind Moscow that he remained in charge even as he began to conform to the Soviet line economically and internationally. If the dismissals indeed discouraged further Soviet-backed internal resistance to his power and policies, his response was reminiscent of his moves against the "microfaction."[21]

CONTROLLING THE MILITARY

The FAR have been the central pillar of the Castro regime, predating the formation of a ruling Communist Party by six years and enjoying a revolutionary legitimacy as the heir to Castro's victorious Rebel Army that still eludes the Party. The FAR has enabled Castro to defeat counterrevolutionary challenges from within and without, and it has given him a global outreach as far as Africa. Although it has served him well, he cannot take the loyalty of the military for granted, because the FAR is changing and undertaking new missions that may endanger its institutional interests.

Safeguards and Counterweights

Castro is well aware that other charismatic Third World leaders—including Sukarno of Indonesia, Ben Bella of Algeria, and Nkrumah of

---

[20] The venerable Carlos Rafael Rodríguez, who continues as a member of the Party's Political Bureau and as a Vice-President in the Councils of Ministers and State, stands out as the major exception. In addition to his intelligence and utility as a more urbane spokesman for the regime, Rodríguez's longevity is due to three factors: First, he was one of two PSP leaders to go to the Sierra Maestra in 1958, and thus established a personal relationship with Castro early on. Second, because of his ties to Castro and prior PSP affiliation, both Havana and Moscow have found him an effective bridge between the two capitals. Third, he retains Soviet support as the Cuban leader representing the more pragmatic, technocratic tendency within the regime.

[21] The regime linked the "microfaction" to Soviet bloc officials. The affair occurred at a time when Castro was facing Soviet economic pressures and his leadership had been weakened—in this instance, by the failure of his revolutionary offensive in Latin America following Guevara's death, and by the worsening economic situation on the island. After the sentencing of 35 members of the "microfaction" to prison, Castro acknowledged that it represented one of "many tendencies" in the revolutionary movement that was "a frankly reformist, reactionary, conservative current." (*Granma Weekly Review*, March 24, 1968, p. 2.)

Ghana—were ousted from power by their own military establishments. He has therefore set up safeguards to ensure the loyalty of the FAR and prevent military conspiracies:

- Since its creation in October 1959, Raúl Castro has headed the FAR as Minister of the MINFAR.
- Within the MINFAR, the General Staff continues to consist of trusted *fidelista* and *raúlista* guerrilla veterans.
- Command of the western, central, and eastern armies has been periodically rotated to preclude the formation of independent regional military chieftainships.
- The FAR's Political Directorate and the high rate of officer membership in the Party are supposed to inculcate proper ideological formation and military loyalty to Castro both as Commander-in-Chief and as PCC First Secretary.
- Until December 1985, the Ministry of Interior was headed by Ramiro Valdés, a *fidelista* loyalist who goes back to the attack on Moncada. He has been succeeded by another guerrilla veteran, Division General José Abrantes Fernández, who served as First Deputy Minister of the Interior under Valdés. Within the Ministry of the Interior (MININT), the Special Troops Battalion serves as Castro's own praetorian guard.

Castro's concern with the military may well have grown in recent years. More than any other organ of government, the FAR has developed its own institutional identity and sense of professionalism, particularly since its successful African campaigns. In addition, the FAR has developed close professional ties with the Soviet military since 1960. Many Cuban officers have received training in the USSR, and the Angolan and especially the Ethiopian operations strengthened the bonds between the two military establishments. In addition, a Soviet Colonel General heads an estimated 2,500 Soviet military advisers in Cuba. As a consequence, the FAR is the most autonomous institution and the one potentially least submissive to Castro's authority. It is potentially the most dangerous as well.

One reason for the rapid expansion of the MTT to 1.5 million members may be that it provides Castro with a counterweight to the FAR, while also enhancing the regime's internal control and national security capabilities.[22] The command and organizational structure of

---

[22]There are probably many reasons for the creation and vast expansion of the MTT. The MTT was initially conceived in 1980 for purposes of social control following the events that led to the Mariel exodus. Then, after the Reagan administration took office, the MTT became a means of further deterring anticipated U.S. aggression. When Castro realized that a U.S. attack on Cuba was unlikely after 1982, he nonetheless accelerated

the MTT even suggests that this is the case:

- Institutionally, the MTT is separate from the FAR; its units are controlled directly by the Party and therefore are responsive to Castro in his capacity as PCC First Secretary.[23]
- Politically, the MTT is tied to Castro because of its mass civilian membership; it also is unencumbered by the organizational autonomy, professional identity, and Soviet ties that characterize the FAR.
- Militarily, the MTT has created a special command for the city of Havana headed by Division General Raúl Menéndez Tomassevich from the FAR, a former guerrilla veteran who served under Castro.
- Rank-and-file members of the MTT have access to light weapons and ammunition and thus can be mobilized on short notice, independent of the regular army.

Hence, although the MTT cannot match the proficiency of the FAR, its very existence may discourage potential coup conspiracies within the military.

Accommodating Institutional Interests

Even as he takes countermeasures, Castro must be careful to satisfy the institutional interests of the FAR. Cuba's successful military campaigns in Africa heightened the professionalism of the FAR, gave it invaluable combat experience, and strengthened the self-esteem and esprit de corps of the Cuban military. The African operations also earned the respect of the Soviet military and enabled the FAR to upgrade its weapon inventory from the Soviet Union. Castro has increased the proportion of the national budget devoted to defense from 9 percent in 1978 and 1979 to 13 percent in 1985. In addition, the officer class is provided with amenities that are less available to the civilian population, including housing, consumer goods, and foodstuffs.

In building up the MTT, however, Castro risks appearing to jeopardize the status of the FAR as Cuba's premier military force. During

---

the expansion of the MTT to fully militarize society, to strengthen Cuba's defenses in the event of either U.S. aggression against Nicaragua or the escalation of the Cuban combat presence in Angola, to economize on Cuba's defenses by trimming conventional forces, and to create a counterweight to the FAR.

[23]As the directing force in Cuban society, the Party controls the MTT through the provincial and municipal PCC First Secretaries who serve as chiefs of the MTT units in their respective provinces and municipalities. Active-duty and retired FAR officers serve in a military training and advisory capacity in the MTT units.

most of 1984, the traditional responsibility of the FAR for national defense was deemphasized, as the MTT was assigned the task of waging a "people's war" under the direction of the Party. Since then, a newly revised military doctrine attempts to integrate the FAR into the people's war by calling upon it to prepare to provide "not only for regular troop action, but also for the struggle of all the people."[24] The proficiency and professionalism of the FAR are acknowledged in that MTT units are to rely on "a contingent of highly qualified [FAR] officers, loyal to the Party and with a high level of political consciousness" for advice and training of MTT cadres.[25] Still, in its section on "the defense of the socialist fatherland," the PCC draft program at the Third Party Congress reaffirmed that the people's war remains the cornerstone of Cuba's "territorial defense system."

The new doctrine reportedly has met with resistance from army officers who may feel that the institutional interests of the FAR are being slighted in favor of the Party-led MTT. This resentment may be further intensified by Cuba's economic austerity measures, which evidently have not affected the MTT but have cut into the FAR's defense budget. The elevation of Division General Abelardo Colomé from alternate status to regular membership in the PCC Political Bureau at the Third Party Congress, and the appointment to the Secretariat of Division General Sixto Batista, formerly Chief of the Central Political Directorate of the FAR, can thus be interpreted either as concessions to the FAR or as steps to ensure the military's subordination to the Party.[26] In either case, civil-military relations show signs of strain.

Potential Divisions and Discontent

At the Third Party Congress, the PCC platform attached a "decisive and growing role" to the political and ideological indoctrination of armed forces personnel in the principles of "Marxism-Leninism, socialist patriotism, and proletarian internationalism." This renewed emphasis on political and ideological correctives suggest that Castro is concerned over the reliability and proficiency of the FAR, a concern initially prompted by the conduct of the Cuban military contingent on Grenada. As with civilian elites, he faces potential generational con-

---

[24]See *Verde Olivo*, December 27, 1984.

[25]*Verde Olivo*, June 13, 1985.

[26]Division Generals Senén Casas Regueiro and Ulises Rosales del Toro were appointed as Political Bureau alternate members as well. Abelardo Colomé's ascendancy over the more senior Senén Casas may be in preparation for his replacement of Raúl Castro as Minister of the FAR at some future date.

flict within the FAR. Another problem stems from the "internationalist" role that he has demanded of the armed forces.

Despite the permanent reassignment of many military officers to civilian posts since 1970, an older generation of guerrilla veterans still occupies the top echelons of the MINFAR and continues to hold the key field commands within the FAR. These guerrilla veterans have positions as First Vice Ministers within the MINFAR (e.g., Division Generals Senén Casas, Colomé,), as Vice Ministers (e.g., Division Generals Julio Casas, García, Ochoa, Rogelio Acevedo), and as Chief of the General Staff (Division General Rosales). Despite more professionalized, advanced training in Cuban and Soviet military schools, and modern combat experience in Angola and Ethiopia, the younger officer class may thus have to await the further retirement of the remaining *fidelista* and *raúlista* officers.

Although the loyalty and commitment of this new post-revolutionary generation is not really in doubt, there have been signs of discontent or unreliability on the part of officers in carrying out their overseas missions. The behavior of the Cuban military contingent on Grenada in October 1983 was particularly revealing—and humiliating to Castro. He had ordered Cuban military personnel and construction workers to fight to the death when U.S. forces invaded the island, presumably in the belief that, by inflicting heavy U.S. casualties, the defense of Grenada might serve to deter the United States from also invading Nicaragua. Although the workers resisted, Colonel Tortoló Cómas and his military staff refused to carry out Castro's order and instead took refuge in the Soviet embassy.

The FAR soon felt the repercussions from Grenada. Because he was responsible for the political awareness of military personnel, Division General Sixto Batista was removed as Chief of the Central Political Directorate of the FAR. More important, in ceremonies that were videotaped for circulation within the military, Colonel Tortoló and his staff were stripped of their ranks and reassigned to combat duty in Angola. Reportedly, some officers considered this staged spectacle an affront to their professionalism. They might also have viewed Castro's demand to fight to the death as irrational and as setting a dangerous precedent for them in future overseas operations.

There was evidence of disaffection on the African front, as well. In January 1985, Lieutenant Colonel Joaquín Mouriño Pérez, a 45-year-old coordinator of Cuban military operations in Africa, defected in Spain because he was unhappy about Cuban soldiers serving as cannon fodder for the Soviet Union.

In sum, the Grenadian losses and the continuing Angolan casualties may have brought home, institutionally and personally, the dangers to the FAR of Cuba's ambitious foreign policy. In particular, the ten-year-old civil war in Angola is a far cry from the glory days of the middle to late 1970s when the victorious Cuban army was seen as the scourge of Africa. Castro must thus take care not to risk alienating the FAR by overextended, high-risk international ventures.

REVIVING THE REVOLUTIONARY COMMITMENT OF THE MASSES

Despite his seeming popularity, Castro may still be uncertain about the extent and depth of his political support. He must recall that, to his bitter surprise, some 125,000 Cubans abandoned the island in the spring and summer of 1980 when the opportunity arose, and several hundred thousand more would have left had he not shut off the escape valve at Mariel in September.[27] With the worsening of the island's economic situation since then, and with the regime acknowledging that the country faces a bleak economic outlook through the year 2000, pressures to emigrate appear to have increased rather than abated.

Concern over the reliability and commitment of sectors of the Cuban masses is suggested by several of Castro's actions over the past two years:

- The buildup of the MTT and the people's war against alleged U.S. aggression created a war psychosis that enabled the regime to maintain the populace in a state of mobilization during the last half of 1984.
- When Radio Martí was formed, the regime quickly installed powerful jamming and counterbroadcast transmitters to block out future transmissions to the island, while also moving to improve the appeal of the regime's own radio programs.
- The signing of the migration agreement with Washington in December 1984 and Castro's subsequent public relations campaign through the U.S. media were undertaken in part with the aim of preventing Radio Martí from going on the air.[28]

---

[27]According to Sánchez Pérez, after the Mariel exodus began, Castro was informed by one of his military officers that more than 2 million Cubans would leave unless he stopped the outflow. (Radio interview with Manuel Sánchez Pérez, Madrid, December 1985.)

[28]This was evident in Castro's reaction just prior to Radio Martí's first transmission: Havana canceled the migration agreement which called for the return of 2,746 Cuban "undesirables" who had arrived in the Mariel exodus of 1980, and for 20,000 Cubans to migrate to the U.S. annually. It also rescinded the 1979 agreement under which Cuban-Americans could visit their families on the island, while also threatening "additional measures relating to communications" between the two countries.

- The Party, *Granma*, *Verde Olivo*, and other organs continue to warn against "ideological diversionism," with *Granma* in early February 1985 condemning desertions from the FAR and negative public attitudes toward military service.

In themselves, these measures do not indicate that the regime is unduly alarmed by the possibility of political unrest. Its pervasive totalitarian controls make dissent difficult and conformity more likely.

Still, Castro evidently is concerned at the growing popularity of Roman Catholicism, Protestantism, and Afro-Cuban sects among segments of the population. This religious revival poses an ideological challenge to the regime: Marxism-Leninism is not satisfying the spiritual and emotional needs of Cuba's increasingly young society; and to the regime's dismay, black and mulatto "internationalists" in Angola have returned to Cuba with a renewed interest in *santería* and other Afro-Cuban cults. Castro has sought to meet this new challenge by establishing the Party's Office of Religious Affairs, meeting with U.S. Catholic bishops, discoursing on religion, and engaging in a "dialogue" with Cuba's Catholic hierarchy in 1985 and 1986.

In seeking to defuse the impact of religion on the Cuban masses, Castro may be entering treacherous ideological ground. At the very least, he must take care not to erode the Marxist-Leninist commitment of the Party faithful by his overtures to the Catholic Church in particular. In the meantime, he is also aware of continued public apathy, low labor productivity, civilian avoidance of military duty, and even military desertions. Hence, Castro cannot afford to ease up on the regime's political controls and mobilization efforts if the revolutionary zeal of the masses is to be maintained.

NEW ECONOMIC PRIORITIES AND URGENCIES

The poor performance of the economy remains Cuba's Achilles' heel, a vulnerability that has been minimized only because of Soviet largess, especially over the past ten years. The poor state of the economy has been a virtual constant since 1960, with only the early 1970s providing a brief respite as a result of booming prices for sugar on the world market. But today Castro faces perhaps even more intractable problems than ever before.

A New Economic Offensive

Prodded by the Soviets, Castro turned public attention to the island's economic situation starting in late 1984. As outlined in the then-secret *Economic Report* from the National Bank of Cuba to Western creditors, dated February 1985, there are five urgent economic priorities that the regime and the people must fulfill during the next five-year plan (1986-1990):[29]

- Increase energy efficiency in order to sell surplus Soviet oil imports on the international market, a practice which Moscow not only permits but evidently encourages.
- Develop new export product lines for Western markets to generate hard-currency revenues needed to meet Cuba's international debt obligations with the West, and to increase Cuba's Western imports.
- Ensure that Cuba honors its export commitments to the socialist countries who thus far have forgiven repeated shortfalls in scheduled exports.
- Accelerate programs of economic development through greater tourism, attraction of foreign investments, acquisition of technologies, and limitations on personal consumption, while "keeping in mind the standard of living already attained by the Cuban people."
- Adjust the investment program as necessary to ensure that the priorities set for the foreign trade sector of the economy are fulfilled.

As in the past, Cuba's traditional export industries—sugar, tobacco, nickel, and citrus—must increase their production as well.

Initially, these priorities were prompted by the poor performance of Cuba's foreign trade sector. According to data supplied by the National Bank of Cuba, export earnings from sales to Western market economies declined sharply, from 22 percent in 1977-80 to 13 percent in 1982-84, due largely to the collapse of world sugar prices. In 1984 alone, exports to the industrialized countries dropped by 26 percent, or nearly 200 million pesos (roughly $220 million, by the official Cuban exchange rate).[30] Also, Moscow's new economic demands on its client-states in the socialist bloc, beginning in 1984, gave additional urgency to Cuba's economic priorities.

---

[29]The Cuban-American National Foundation, *Cuba's Financial Crisis: The Secret Report from the National Bank of Cuba*, Washington, D.C., 1985 (hereafter cited as *Secret Report*), pp. 3-5. This report was submitted by the Banco Nacional de Cuba to Cuba's Western creditors—banks and governments—in February 1985 as part of the Cuban government's efforts to renegotiate $726.7 million of its $3.3 billion debt to the West. Made available by a West European source, the authenticity of the *Secret Report* has been confirmed.

[30]*Secret Report*, pp. 3, 13.

Economic and Political Impediments

Despite his new economic campaign and exhortations to the contrary, Castro realizes that Cuba faces severe limitations in trying to revitalize its economy. Thus, whereas his regime claims that the 1985 overall growth rate for the economy was 4.8 percent, measured in terms of Global Social Product (GSP), the 1986 projection is a more modest 3.0 to 3.5 percent, while individual consumption is projected to grow at an even slower rate of 2.5 to 3.0 percent.[31] In his Report to the Third Party Congress, Castro listed a catalog of economic ills, complaining that, among other things:

> There are still some subjective conditions in the national economy that conspire against reducing production costs, increasing profitability and saving material, labor and financial resources.
>
> Shortages of all kinds of packaging consistently affected several production lines; as a result, export commitments were not met and supplies were not delivered to the population.
>
> Cost effectiveness is still hampered by idle raw materials, spare parts and other goods and resources frozen because of problems in planning and administering supplies.
>
> One of our most serious problems has been the absence of comprehensive national planning for economic development, particularly where individual sectors have planned and executed investments on their own initiative without adequate centralized control. Examples abound.[32]

Some of Cuba's problems arise from natural causes or are of a structural nature beyond the regime's capacity to control. But most others, described below, are of Castro's own choosing.

Poor outlook for export earnings. Cuba's major export commodities, particularly sugar, have faced severely depressed international prices. There is the possibility that the so-called "six-year cycle" in the world market price of sugar may cause a significant upturn in 1986, as

---

[31]*Granma Weekly Review*, January 12, 1986, pp. 3, 4, and 8. As used in the Soviet bloc planned economies, GSP should not be confused with the Western concept of Gross National Product (GNP): GSP is derived by a different methodology which includes double-accounting, and it cannot be compared with the GNP performance of Western economies.

[32]The examples include "new industries and agricultural projects in sparsely populated areas lacking housing facilities for the labor force; extremely important agricultural plans, such as the citrus fruit plan, where we still have areas planted without irrigation; irrigation systems where there are no pumping stations or electric power to run them; workshops and facilities without the corresponding power supply; housing developments completed without the necessary urban infrastructure, etc." (*Granma Weekly Review*, February 16, 1986, p. 6.)

occurred in 1974 when sugar prices briefly reached a record high of 65 cents per pound, and in 1980 when prices rose again, although far less spectacularly. Because drought conditions have cut into Brazilian sugar production, there is thus some expectation that higher prices will recur in 1986.

However, Cuba may not be in a position to take advantage of a rise in world sugar prices due to its own expected harvest shortfall. The 1985 drought—rain did not fall during the first half of the year—adversely affected the island's sugar production. Then, just as the sugar fields were recovering and the harvest was about to begin, Hurricane Kate struck, causing serious damage to the sugarcane.[33] Cuba's capacity to earn hard currency on the rising world market may be further restricted by its large sugar export commitments to the Soviet Union, unless the Soviets substantially reduce those obligations. In the meantime, Cuba's reexport of Soviet-supplied petroleum will now yield lower revenues than it has in the past, because of the sharp decline in world crude oil prices.

Integration into the socialist camp. Because 85 percent of its foreign trade is now with the socialist camp and trade commitments with the Soviet bloc have already been signed for the remainder of the 1980s, the Cuban economy has very little leeway for increasing its exports to the industrialized West. As Castro himself has conceded, Cuba would be unable to take advantage of trade with the United States even if Washington were to reverse its policies.[34] In the meantime, its integration into the Eastern bloc system leaves Cuba highly dependent upon shoddy Soviet-made goods and second-rate technology—including nuclear energy technology.[35]

---

[33]In his speech to the closing session of the National Assembly of People's Power, held in December 1985, Castro was reported as saying that "never before had he seen sugarcane so seriously damaged by winds and that the destruction caused by the hurricane was incalculable." (*Granma Weekly Review*, January 12, 1986, p. 5.)

[34]"Frankly, the United States has fewer and fewer things to offer Cuba. If we were able to export our products to the United States, we would have to start making plans for new lines of production to be exported to the United States, because *everything we are producing now and everything we are going to produce in the next five years has already been sold to other markets.* We would have to take them away from other socialist countries in order to sell them to the United States, and the socialist countries pay us much better prices and have better relations with us than does the United States [emphasis added]." ("Playboy Interview," p. 179.)

[35]The Soviet Union is completing the installation of two nuclear reactors near Cienfuegos, the first of which is scheduled to begin operation by 1990. They are of a different design than the reactor at the Chernobyl nuclear station in the Ukraine that experienced a major accident in April 1986. Still, Cubans must now have second thoughts about the Soviet commitment to nuclear safety, despite Castro's earlier assurances. In December 1984, he scoffed at the possibility of a nuclear accident in Cuba, claiming that such a problem is limited to capitalist countries "seeking to cut corners and costs." "Fortu-

Disinterest by Western investors. In a heretical move, the Castro regime enacted new legislation in 1982 intended to attract foreign investments from any country.[36] But Cuba remains unattractive to Western investors because of its politicized, mismanaged, and highly centralized economy, its inefficient labor force, and its international behavior. Thus, Cuba will probably remain cut off from the infusions of Western capital, technology, and marketing ties it needs to expand its economy as part of the world economy, unless the regime radically alters its economic philosophy and institutions. But Castro and his followers are not likely to follow the example of China under Deng Xiaoping.

Reliance on political solutions. For Castro, economic problems are almost invariably infused with political content, and the politics generally take priority over economic rationality.[37] Today, as in the past, he resists the institutionalization of economic policymaking and market mechanisms not just for ideological reasons, but because they would diminish his own power within the regime and his regime's control over society. Conversely, he relies upon political solutions to solve what are essentially economic or technical problems.

At the end of 1984, for instance, he disregarded Humberto Pérez and JUCEPLAN by appointing Osmani Cienfuegos, who has no economic training but is a veteran troubleshooter and member of the Political Bureau, to reconcile the budget for 1985 with the regime's new economic priorities. Further emphasis on political solutions results from the "guiding role" played by the Party at virtually all levels of the economy. Through its network of PCC cells at the local and enterprise levels, the Party is thus called upon "to exert control over the country's economic development."[38]

As in the 1960s, political mobilization and exhortation is at the heart of Castro's call for "the economic war of the whole people." At the National Assembly of People's Power at the end 1985, he (and

---

nately," he went on, "we rely on Soviet technology," adding that "all the responsibility the socialist state can muster goes into technological progress with safety." (*The New York Times*, May 1, 1986, p. 8.)

[36]The March 1982 investment law provides for joint ventures with the state, allowing private or public foreign companies up to 49 percent ownership, and offers tax incentives, profit remittance, labor, and other inducements to foreign investors.

[37]For example, his sweeping nationalization decrees of the early 1960s had the primary political objective of destroying the American-linked Cuban bourgeoisie, or middle class. His "Revolutionary Offensive" of April 1968, which nationalized what remained of the privately owned nonagrarian sector, also was aimed in large part at realizing socialism and communism simultaneously, rather than sequentially over decades.

[38]José Ramón Machado Ventura, "The Growth of the Party's Leading Role in the Life of Cuban Society," *Partiynaya Zhizn*, November 21, 1985, pp. 75-76. Machado Ventura is a member of the PCC Political Bureau and Secretariat.

other speakers) also stressed administrative and legal remedies rather than economic and other incentive systems for dealing with the persistent problems of worker absenteeism and lack of labor discipline.[39] Similarly, at the Third Party Congress in February 1986, he delivered a harsh indictment of inefficiency and bureaucratism, warning, "There will be no tolerance whatsoever for laziness, negligence, incompetence or irresponsibility. The apprentice stage must be left behind once and for all."[40] Two months later, on the twenty-fifth anniversary of Playa Girón, he lashed out against those in and outside the regime who "shamefully play at capitalism," while threatening to "hurl the masses against those responsible for such irritating deeds."[41]

Resistance to liberalization. The economy might begin to recover if the regime adopted structural reforms that decentralized planning and economic activities and provided economic incentives, through the kinds of market mechanisms employed in Hungary and China. But for reasons of power and ideology, Castro has worked to limit administrative as well as liberalizing reforms, including those pushed by the Soviets.[42]

In 1980, for example, Castro permitted the introduction of reforms that granted greater wage differentials and bonuses as incentives for managers and workers to raise factory production. But as one observer has noted, "Often the stimuli are not strong enough, and in other cases [they] conflict with politically or ideologically motivated priorities and policies."[43] Indeed, in his Playa Girón speech of April 19, 1986, Castro condemned those state directors who had converted their plants into capitalist-type enterprises, demanding instead that they ask "not whether their enterprise profits more, but whether the country will profit more."[44]

Castro's position on the free peasant market provides still further evidence of his opposition to liberalizing reforms that may erode his socialist vision—and his ability to control Cuban behavior. In 1980, he

---

[39] See *Granma Weekly Review*, January 12, 1986, p. 6.

[40] *Granma Weekly Review*, February 16, 1986, p. 8.

[41] *Granma Resumen Semanal*, April 27, 1986, pp. 9–10.

[42] According to Manuel Sánchez Pérez, the former Vice Minister of the State Committee for Material and Technical Supply, Humberto Pérez was initially viewed as the regime's "golden boy," but "failed because he was not permitted to continue with the [Soviet-style] policy changes which might have represented a relatively greater increase in efficiency within the Cuban economy." (Radio interview with Manuel Sánchez Pérez, Madrid, December 1985.)

[43] Carmelo Mesa-Lago, "The Economy: Caution, Frugality, and Resilient Ideology," in Jorge I. Domínguez, *Cuba: Internal and International Affairs*, Sage Publications, Beverly Hills, 1982, p. 155.

[44] *Granma Resumen Semanal*, April 27, 1986, p. 9

allowed the introduction of a free peasant market to stimulate the production of foodstuffs that for years had been unavailable to Cuba's hard-pressed consumers. Initially, farmers were allowed to sell produce at whatever prices they could command after first meeting their government quotas. In 1982, after criticizing the enrichment of peasants, Castro imposed new restrictions on their sales and a 20 percent tax on their profits. Then, a month after his Playa Girón speech, he abolished the six-year experiment with the free peasant market, denouncing it as "a source of enrichment for neo-capitalists and neo-bourgeois."[45] Indeed, Castro today appears to be striving to return to his radicalism of the pre-1970 period, with its heightened emphasis on revolutionary morality, socialist ethics, and social control.

To be sure, some aspects of Cuba's command economy may be relaxed, as with the 1985 housing law that attempts to ease the island's severe housing shortage by encouraging tenants to purchase their dwellings and rent out rooms. Yet, Castro (along with his brother) is certain to rule out structural reforms that would significantly alter the socialist character of the Cuban economy and its concentrations of political power. As evidenced by his Playa Girón speech, this means continued opposition to administrative decentralization that would empower enterprises and local municipalities with the authority to allocate scarce resources, or measures that would introduce a realistic pricing system and monetary incentives for the operation of the state-run economy. On these issues, he may be supported by elements in the central bureaucracy who evidently wish greater decisionmaking autonomy for themselves but want to deny it to others.[46] He is even less likely to permit any denationalization of the economy that would restore private control over key sectors of production.[47]

---

[45]*The New York Times*, May 20, 1986, p. 6. Castro aimed his attack at the middlemen who purchased commodities from farmers and resold them at a profit in the cities.

[46]In late February and March 1985, *Granma* reported that the central ministries were resisting the devolution of decisionmaking authority to enterprise managers and were relying instead upon on greater bureaucratic controls to ensure performance. Before his departure from JUCEPLAN, Humberto Pérez also criticized managers for continuing to emphasize physical output measures rather than taking cost and profitability into account when trying to fulfill production targets. Resistance to decentralization and market mechanisms thus has systemic as well as Castro-derived causes.

[47]Although the new housing law permits tenants to purchase their homes from the state and rent out rooms, it does not affect the "commanding heights of the economy," which remain under state ownership or control. Individuals are limited to buying their house or apartment unit and a second vacation home for limited use; they cannot invest in real estate, which remains the preserve of the state. Similarly, the formation of thrift institutions in 1985, which are to pay about 2 percent interest to depositors, does not alter the highly socialized character of the Cuban economy.

The Soviet Union remains the major question mark for Castro and his regime. Moscow—especially under the Gorbachev regime—has been pushing Havana to raise the efficiency and productive capacity of the Cuban economy, to become less wasteful of Soviet economic assistance and trade subsidies, and to meet Cuba's trade commitments to the socialist bloc. While Cuba may take its cue from the Soviets, it remains to be seen whether the Gorbachev regime itself will go beyond the mere reorganization of ministries and the introduction of automation and new technologies to the implementation of liberalizing measures that would reorient the Soviet economy along lines of the Hungarian model.[48] Until that occurs, it is doubtful that Cuban technocrats will be able to achieve economic liberalization in Cuba. Over the short to medium term, Castro is not likely to be compelled to alter fundamentally the character of the Cuban economy.

ORCHESTRATING LEADERSHIP CHANGE: TURNING TO RAÚL

During much of 1985, Castro appeared to be grooming his brother Raúl to take a larger administrative role in the running of the Cuban government and economy. But although he was reinstalled as Second Secretary at the Third Party Congress and formally designated as Castro's successor, Raúl was not appointed to a new governmental post. Whether or not he is formally given such a post, it appears virtually certain that he will play a more direct administrative role in the not too distant future.

For years in the shadow of his brother, Raúl Castro has earned a reputation as an effective administrator as Minister of the FAR. Because he is a reliable political-bureaucratic *apparatchik* rather than a free-wheeling charismatic leader, he also enjoys good standing in Moscow, which he visits frequently. Yet, he appears to be utterly loyal to his older brother, to the extent that he continues to be second-in-command of Cuba's ruling institutions in his multiple roles as Second Secretary of the PCC, First Vice-President of both the Council of Ministers and Council of State, and head of the armed forces. Over and above these formal positions, Fidel has entrusted Raúl with building up the FAR, militarizing society through the MTT, and dealing with the Soviet and Eastern bloc governments. It was Raúl who substituted for

---

[48]For a report on unemployment created by the Soviet modernization efforts, see *The New York Times*, January 9, 1986, pp. 1, 6. On the possibility of structural reforms, see Stephen F. Cohen, "Gorbachev's Gamble," *Los Angeles Times*, January 12, 1985, Sec. V, p. 5.

Fidel at the funeral of Konstantine Chernenko and who thus met with Gorbachev in March 1985.

As Raúl's scope of activities visibly broadened during 1985, speculation arose that he would assume a greater role in the administration of national affairs.[49] This could still occur in 1986 and beyond if Fidel (1) strengthens Raúl's role as First Vice-President of the Council of Ministers, (2) creates a new, special overseer role for Raúl as Prime Minister, or (3) resigns his post as President of the Council of Ministers and turns it over to Raúl.[50] Fidel could turn to Raúl to improve Cuba's economic performance, to mollify Moscow, or to relieve himself of tiresome administrative duties—and of responsibility for future economic setbacks. Such a political solution to the economic crisis would preserve his power while enabling him to devote more of his attention to the world stage.

The departure in 1985 of three veteran *fidelistas* from the Council of Ministers may have been partly designed to pave the way for Raúl to assume the reins of government in 1986. All three men were dismissed because of unsatisfactory performance.[51] Then at the Third Party Congress, they were also dropped from the ruling Political Bureau. They were replaced by two of Raúl's followers (his ex-wife, Vilma Espín, and Division General Abelardo Colomé), which should strengthen his position in both the Party and government.

Should Raúl take over the running of the government and replace some of the previously untouchable *historicos*, the new second-rank subordinates will be more easily held accountable for the performance of their government ministries. Further dismissals will also facilitate the rise of a younger generation of leaders. In the meantime, the

---

[49] Raúl gained greater public prominence on the pages of *Granma* and the rest of the Cuban media, frequently toured the provinces in a fact-finding capacity, engaged in grass-roots pulse-taking throughout the island, and attended numerous Party meetings and conferences both in and outside military.

[50] The last is probably the least likely alternative, given Castro's disinclination to give up or share political power, even if the office is vested with essentially an administrative function. With a visit to Cuba by Pope John Paul II still a possibility, Castro is probably even less inclined to remove one of his hats.

[51] In June 1985, Guillermo García was replaced as Minister of Transportation following public revelations in *Granma* and elsewhere regarding chronic deficiencies in the performance of his ministry. In early December, Ramiro Valdés was relieved as Minister of the Interior in the wake of reports concerning corruption and scandals involving MININT intelligence personnel abroad. There was also speculation that he had resisted Castro's new line toward the Catholic Church, which is consistent with Valdés's reputation as a militant hardliner. Given new duties in the electronics industry area, he was succeeded by his First Vice-Minister, Division General José Abrantes Fernández. Later in December, Sergio del Valle asked that he be replaced as Minister of Public Health by someone with greater technical knowledge and organizational competence. He was succeeded by his First Vice-Minister, Julio Teja Pérez.

removal of *fidelista* leaders from the day-to-day administration of the government could help to shield Castro's authority and the *fidelista* mystique during a period of renewed hardship, austerity, and regimentation for the Cuban public.[52]

Raúl's ascension and the strengthening of the *raúlista* representation in the Political Bureau should placate Soviet demands for greater managerial efficiency and rationality in the administration of the Cuban economy. This factor alone is likely to ease the strain in Soviet-Cuban relations that was evident in 1984-85, and assure that adequate levels of Soviet economic assistance will be forthcoming. In his address to the Third Party Congress, the head of the Soviet delegation, Politburo member Yegor Ligachev, hinted as much. He noted "with satisfaction" that the Cuban Communists were speaking openly not only about their successes, but also about "shortcomings and problems that are still awaiting solution." He commended the PCC for recognizing the "key importance" of economic matters in the development of socialist societies, noting with approval that Cuba now had a "realistic economic strategy."[53]

What role will Castro play if his younger brother assumes greater control over internal affairs? In all probability, he will concentrate his attention on the world stage, not only because internal administrative matters interest him less, but also because it is on the international front that he may be able to bolster his sagging leadership image, coalesce the regime around him, and revitalize the Cuban people's revolutionary élan.

---

[52]If he is given greater governmental authority, Raúl is likely to find it difficult to revive the Cuban economy. He must still overcome structural problems, his own ideological rigidity, and his brother's omnipresence as Cuba's *caudillo*.

[53]*TASS*, Moscow, February 5, 1986.

V. CASTRO AND THE WORLD

With the Third Party Congress now behind him, Castro faces an international environment that is virtually the reverse of what it was when the First Party Congress met in late 1975. At that time, his regime was still riding high from a boom in world sugar prices; it had broken out of its diplomatic isolation in Latin America; and it felt secure because of détente and other constraints acting on the United States in the post-Vietnam period. Believing that the international correlation of forces was shifting against the West, Castro intervened in Angola and later in Ethiopia, and afterward assumed leadership of the Non-Aligned Movement. By the start of the present decade, he had successfully exploited the internationalization of conflict in the Caribbean Basin to gain new Marxist-Leninist allies in Grenada and Nicaragua, and was actively supporting the Salvadoran insurgency.[1]

Today Castro sees that Grenada is gone, Nicaragua is under siege, and international conditions are not as favorable as they were only five years ago. Shifts in the international correlation of forces have created uncertainties as to which superpower, the United States or the Soviet Union, is becoming stronger and which side will win the long-term global struggle. While opportunities exist for new Cuban gains, they also are more limited and/or fraught with greater risks than in the late 1970s, when Castro was aggressively pursuing his maximalist ambitions. His current world view and the trends he is likely to see are now more ambiguous and disturbing.

The positions of both superpowers limit the opportunities for Cuban activism abroad, and both their policies pose greater risks for Castro. He is finding that neither superpower is susceptible to his manipulations, that his own patron has become more demanding of his regime, and that the United States is more inclined to actively challenge his and other radical regimes in the Third World.

Since Grenada, the possibilities for further Cuban-Soviet advances have receded in Central America and the Caribbean, while Cuba's clients are under attack. Having previously embarked upon the path of revolutionary expansionism, the growth of indigenous insurgencies in Angola and Nicaragua is now likely to raise the costs and risks to Castro of assuring the survival of his client regimes in these states.

---

[1]On the internationalization of conflict in Central America, see David Ronfeldt, *Geopolitics, Security, and U.S. Strategy in the Caribbean Basin*, The Rand Corporation, R-2997-AF/RC, November 1983; and James LeMoyne, "The Guerrilla Network," *The New York Times Magazine*, April 6, 1986.

Mounting internal and international opposition to apartheid in South Africa may cause Castro to renew his political-military offensive in southern Africa, but it also poses heightened risks for Cuba. He now faces more constraints on the employment of Cuban military power abroad, not only because of international considerations but also for domestic reasons.

A more complex and fractious Third World is evolving that is less uniformly militant, with the result that Castro is less able to forge unity and attract allies. He is confronted with the ascendancy of capitalist-oriented newly industrializing countries in Asia, the resurgence of democracy in Latin America, and the emergence of Islamic fundamentalism. He finds that he must share the world stage with rival charismatic or more youthful leaders who challenge his claim to leadership of the Third World.

In line with these trends, Castro is thus temporarily constrained from pursuing a maximalist course. He has shifted tactically to a more prudent posture, exploiting less risky developments such as the Latin American debt and fissures within the Catholic Church. But his mindset prevents him from reaching an accommodation with the United States, ceasing his "anti-imperialist" struggle, or openly abandoning his clients in Nicaragua and Angola. Beyond the immediate future, therefore, he will probably search anxiously for new openings in the Third World by which to refurbish his leadership image at home and abroad.

CUBA AND THE INTERNATIONAL CORRELATION OF FORCES

Castro has always been attentive to shifts in "the international correlation of forces," a phrase he has used since the early 1960s. In his assessment of the forces at work in the international environment, the following broad questions become central to his regime's security and the realization of his international ambitions:

- Who is becoming stronger in the East-West struggle?
- What opportunities are available in the North-South struggle?

These two issues are closely intertwined in Castro's general assessment of the international environment and the opportunities for Cuban foreign policy.

Castro's perspective depends on carefully weighing the strengths of the two superpowers and their respective dispositions toward Cuba and contested Third World areas, and then identifying targets of opportunity in the Caribbean Basin, Latin America, and elsewhere in the Third World. He has long believed that a Cuban role in world affairs can affect the correlation of forces and the outcome of the international struggle. Thus, Cuba may become most interventionist when Castro considers the international opportunity factor to be optimal in terms of four basic conditions:

- *When U.S. power is effectively neutralized.* In the post-Vietnam era, weakened U.S. resolve, U.S. global disengagement, and détente all shielded Cuba from U.S. reprisals during Cuba's period of heightened "internationalist" activities.
- *When the Soviet Union is in an expansionist mode.* Starting in the mid-1970s, the Soviets became willing to exploit, directly and indirectly through Cuba, new openings in the Third World to extend Soviet influence in Africa, the Middle East, Central America, and Grenada.
- *When winnable targets of opportunity exist in the Third World.* Exploiting events, Cuba intervened militarily in Angola and Ethiopia and stepped up its assistance to the Sandinista Front of National Liberation (FSLN) in Nicaragua, the Bishop regime in Grenada, and the FMLN in El Salvador.
- *When Cuban intervention can be legitimized.* Ever concerned with justifying Cuban actions according to higher principles while minimizing the possibility of U.S. retaliation, Cuba claimed it could intervene in Angola because of South Africa's initial presence, in Ethiopia because of Somalian aggression, and in Nicaragua because of Latin American opposition to Somoza.

Accordingly, the Third World becomes the operational target of Castro's ambitions, but he keys his operations to the positions of the United States and especially the Soviet Union.

SHIFTS IN THE EAST-WEST STRUGGLE

Castro's first concern today is the course of the East-West struggle and its effect on the international correlation of forces. He will remain attentive to who is getting stronger and who weaker, and who seems to be winning and who losing the global struggle between East and West. Although he remains steadfast in his convictions that socialist forces will ultimately prevail, he must be concerned about recent trends.

A Stronger, More Aggressive United States

In watching and weighing U.S. foreign policy behavior across almost three decades, Castro appears to be particularly sensitive to three aspects that are fairly indicative of his overall assessment:

- The domestic and international constraints on the application of U.S. military power abroad.
- The divisions and lack of consensus in U.S. Congressional and public opinion about U.S. roles abroad.
- Castro's ability to engage each administration in a disarming dialogue about potential accommodation.

In recent years, Castro has shown that he can badly misjudge these aspects in his reading of the American political scene. In fact, events during the Reagan administration have diminished his prior optimism in each respect.

Fewer constraints on U.S. power. The Reagan administration has revived a "rollback" strategy against Communism, as seen by the intervention in Grenada and the support for anti-Communist insurgencies in Nicaragua and Angola. Although the memory of Vietnam lingers on, making the U.S. public anxious about, if not opposed to, "militarized" solutions, the Grenadian operation in October 1983 won widespread public favor. Two years later, public reaction to the U.S. air intercept of the Palestinian hijackers of the Achille Lauro, and especially to the U.S. airstrikes against Libya in March and April 1986, have confirmed that the administration can rally the American people behind the employment of military power. Indeed, judging from his regime's shrill condemnation, Castro must be concerned about the implications of the U.S. actions against Khaddafi for Nicaragua and even Cuba itself.[2]

A greater policy consensus. Castro knows that the Reagan administration is not alone. A new anti-Communist as well as anti-terrorist mood has also emerged in the U.S. Congress, encompassing both political parties. This is evidenced by the repeal of the Clark Amendment

---

[2]In an April 15, 1986, editorial statement that suggested Castro's own hand, the daily edition of *Granma* charged, among other things, that "Washington is the center for state terrorism against the emancipated peoples, with headquarters in the White House and Ronald Reagan as its chief ringleader"; that it employs "rhetoric reminiscent of Goebbels," and that President Reagan should be branded as an "international criminal." (Reprinted in *Granma Weekly Review*, April 20, 1986, p. 1.) In his Playa Girón speech, Castro repeatedly accused President Reagan of being "the legitimate heir of Hitler" because the U.S. attack on Tripoli was meant to kill Khaddafi, while further charging that the Tripoli attack was no different from the bombings of Warsaw, Amsterdam, and London during World War II. (*Granma Resumen Semanal*, April 27, 1986, p. 8.)

and the authorization of nonmilitary aid to the Contras in June 1985, both of which reversed previous equivocations by moderate and even liberal members of Congress. Hence, Castro is certain to watch closely the final outcome of the Congressional debate on the $100 million military and nonmilitary aid package to the Contras that is expected to resume later in 1986.

A less manipulative political process. In the past, Castro has been able to promote a disarming dialogue about potential U.S.-Cuban accommodation that he has used to curry favor in U.S. media and Congressional circles and put successive U.S. administrations on the defensive. He has failed to succeed with this tactic during the Reagan administration, as the U.S. political process has become less susceptible to manipulation by Havana and its allies. Castro's signing of a U.S.-Cuban migration agreement in December 1984 and his extraordinary media blitz in the months that followed failed to prevent the Reagan administration from putting Radio Martí on the air in May 1985. Meanwhile, public relations blunders by other Third World actors—particularly Libya and Nicaragua—have also worked to the administration's advantage and Cuba's disadvantage.[3]

At the very least, these developments in the "Colossus of the North" must be unsettling to Castro. By carefully modulating his activities, he has long succeeded in avoiding U.S. military action against his country. Now, however, he must be concerned that Cuba remains the most exposed salient of the Soviet Union's extended empire at a time when the Reagan administration has strengthened American military might and employed it against Grenada and Libya. In the event of an East-West crisis in Europe, the Middle East, Africa, or the Caribbean Basin, Cuba could become a likely target because of its close military ties with the Soviets and its potential threat to critical U.S. sea lanes of communication in the Basin.[4] For the same reason, the probabilities are even greater that a U.S. attack on Cuba could occur in the context of a U.S.-Nicaraguan crisis. Castro knows that such scenarios are no longer idle speculations with this U.S. administration.

---

[3]In the Nicaraguan case, for example, President Daniel Ortega's visit to Moscow immediately following the initial Congressional vote denying aid to the Contras in April 1985 helped reverse that vote the following June.

[4]On the potential military threat posed by Cuba, see Gonzalez, *A Strategy for Dealing with Cuba in the 1980s*, pp. 3–25; and R. Bruce McColm, "Central America and the Caribbean: The Larger Scenario," *Strategic Review*, Summer 1983, pp. 28–42. On the strategic importance of the region to U.S. security interests, see David Ronfeldt, *Geopolitics, Security, and U.S. Strategy in the Caribbean Basin*.

A Tougher but More Cautious Soviet Union

For Castro, Cuba's relationship with the Soviet Union has not only served to guarantee his regime's survival, it has also been the single most important external factor in defining Cuba's international role. Over the past decade or so, Castro's behavior indicates that he pays close attention to:

- Soviet-bloc support for the Cuban economy.
- Soviet military expansionism and/or support for revolution in the Third World, with Cuba playing a strong allied role.
- The presence of Soviet political leaders supportive of Castro's views.

In each respect, Castro faces new uncertainties, particularly since Gorbachev's appointment as General Secretary of the CPSU.

New economic concerns. The Gorbachev regime must wrestle with economic and administrative inefficiencies in virtually all sectors of the Soviet economy. The new program for the Communist Party provides a surprisingly bleak assessment and projects only modest achievements for the next 15 years, thereby prolonging the calendar for fully achieving the promises of communism. Partly as a result, Moscow already appears less forgiving and more demanding of its client-states in Eastern Europe. The Gorbachev regime is pressing Eastern bloc governments to adhere to centralized economic planning and control, fulfill their trade commitments with the Soviet Union, supply better quality goods, and invest in Soviet oil and gas industries.[5]

The implications for Cuba are not clear, but Gorbachev's new emphasis on economic productivity may mean less Soviet largess for the Cuban economy. This may help to explain why Castro has given top priority to Cuba's pressing economic problems and its need to meet its export commitments to the Soviet bloc and the West. Cuba's past track record, however, gives Moscow good reason to doubt the efficacy of Castro's newest campaign. Negative assessments of Cuban economic performance may be reinforced by the first-hand knowledge by two former Soviet ambassadors to Cuba who are now close allies of Gorbachev and who hold important positions in Moscow, Vitallii Ivanovich Vorotnikov and Konstantin Katushev.

---

[5]The new Soviet line was highlighted by a major article in *Pravda* on June 21, 1985. (See the comprehensive report by Robert Gillette in the *Los Angeles Times*, August 26, 1985.) For a further analysis, see Harry Gelman, "East Europe as an Inhibiting Factor for Soviet Policy: Prospects for the Next Decade," paper prepared for the European American Institute for Security Research workshop on "Fault Lines in the Soviet Empire: Implications for Western Security (II)," held at St.-Jean-Cap-Ferrat, France, September 16–18, 1985.

Restraint regarding Third World commitments. Another important uncertainty for Castro is the commitment of the new Soviet leadership to an expansionist foreign policy that matches his ambitions—and might even follow his lead. The period of the mid-1970s to early 1980s saw considerable coincidence between Havana and Moscow in this respect because of the Soviet Union's expansionist surge in Africa, the Middle East, and the Caribbean Basin. But recent Soviet behavior in the Basin cannot be reassuring to him.[6]

In Grenada, the Soviet Union and its allies (Czechoslovakia, East Germany, North Korea, Vietnam, and Cuba) signed secret agreements with the new Marxist-Leninist regime of Maurice Bishop for the supply of weapons and military-security assistance. Nevertheless, the Grenada papers show that the Bishop government "received a back-of-the-hand treatment from Soviet political authorities. Its relationship with Soviet officials was confined to low-level functionaries."[7] Moreover, Moscow may have worked at cross-purposes to Havana even before it abandoned the island and Cuban forces to the U.S. invasion. The Soviets reacted suspiciously to Bishop's confidential meeting with then National Security Adviser William Clark in spring 1983.[8] In the months that followed, Soviet backing for Bishop evidently cooled, even though Castro himself personally threw his support behind his protégé prior to the power struggle that consumed the New Jewel Movement.[9] At worst, Moscow may have cultivated and encouraged the Coard faction to depose Bishop along the lines of an "Afghanistan Solution."[10]

---

[6]On the convergence and divergence of Soviet interests with those of Cuba in the region, see Gonzalez, "The Cuban and Soviet Challenge in the Caribbean Basin," pp. 73–94.

[7]Paul Seabury and Walter A. McDougall (eds.), *The Grenada Papers*, San Francisco: Institute of Contemporary Studies, 1984, p. 182.

[8]In Moscow, a Foreign Ministry official queried the Grenadian Ambassador at length concerning Bishop's meeting with Clark, insisting that it would have been courteous of the Grenadian government to have informed the Soviets of the visit. (See the confidential report by the Grenadian Ambassador, W. Richard Jacobs, July 11, 1983, in Seabury and McDougall (eds.), *The Grenada Papers*, p. 205.)

[9]Before returning to Grenada after his trip to Eastern Europe in October 1983, Bishop stopped over in Havana. He was given a high-level reception by Castro, attended by Raúl and six other members of the PCC Political Bureau, allegedly as a show of support. Immediately after Bishop's arrest, Castro wrote to the New Jewel Movement's Central Committee and indignantly condemned as "a miserable piece of slander" the notion that Cuba would meddle in Grenadian affairs, insisting, "We are people of principle, not vulgar schemers or adventurers." (See "Letter from Castro to Central Committee, 10/15/83," and "Letter from Noel to Central Committee, 10/17/83," in Seabury and McDougal (eds.), *The Grenada Papers*, pp. 327, 334.)

[10]On Soviet ties with the Coard faction and Moscow's reaction to the coup and murder of Bishop, see Jiri and Virginia Valenta, "Leninism in Grenada," *Problems of Communism*, July-August 1984, pp. 20–22. In his October 17th letter to the New Jewel Movement's Central Committee, Vincent Noel relates that Bishop, upon return from his

In Nicaragua, Moscow has recently increased its military and economic aid to the struggling Sandinista regime in an apparent bid to keep the regime from collapsing. But the $200 million in Soviet bloc credits extended to President Daniel Ortega in April 1985 came before the tougher anti-Communist mood emerged in the U.S. Congress. Since then, the Soviets have continued to provide the military wherewithal for Nicaragua's aspiring Marxist-Leninist regime to defend itself against internal and external opposition. In fact, Moscow has gone so far as to supply Managua with heavy weapons, including the MI-24 helicopter gunship for use in counter-insurgency operations. Nonetheless, as with Grenada, the Soviets have not recognized Nicaragua as a Communist-run state that is in the stage of "building socialism," thus carefully limiting its political, economic, and military commitments to Managua.[11] As a consequence, it is Cuba that has the greater stake in Nicaragua, with Castro identifying himself with the Sandinista regime to the extent of assigning Cuban military advisers to the battalion light infantry units doing battle with the Contras.

Castro must now be all the more concerned over mounting signs that Moscow is reassessing Soviet policy and interests in the Third World, and may be entering a period of retrenchment and consolidation there, or, at best, selective engagement.[12] He sees that Moscow appears preoccupied not only with its economic problems, but also with the civil war in Afghanistan, a range of difficulties in Eastern Europe, and the larger strategic issues concerning the United States following the Reagan-Gorbachev summit meeting in November 1985. Indeed, Soviet activism in much of the Third World could be further constrained if Moscow gives highest priority to stabilizing its relationship with Washington. In this respect, Castro must have found it profoundly disturbing that Gorbachev failed to offer traditional Kremlin pledges of support to "wars of national liberation" and "liberation

---

East European trip, had expressed his fears that an "Afghanistan Solution" would be attempted in Grenada, as had occurred in Afghanistan when Moscow sought to replace one Communist regime with another more reliable one. (See Seabury and McDougal (eds.), *The Grenada Papers*, pp. 331–334.)

[11]Even with their arms transfers and other forms of military assistance, the Soviets have been careful: "The Soviets have demonstrated a clear preference for using intermediaries in the delivery of arms (at least until now): indeed, not only such trusted allies as Bulgaria, East Germany, and Cuba, but seemingly more neutral shippers, like Algeria, have been utilized when possible. Although there is a large Cuban advisory presence in Managua, the Soviets themselves have some 200 military and civilian advisers—a far cry from the numbers of advisers in Angola or Mozambique, for example." (Peter Clement, "Moscow and Nicaragua: Two Sides of Soviet Policy," *Comparative Strategy*, Vol. 5, No. 1, 1985, p. 82.)

[12]See the extensive analysis by Frank Fukuyama, *Moscow's Post-Brezhnev Reassessment of the Third World*, The Rand Corporation, R-3337-USDP, February 1986.

struggles" in his keynote address to the Twenty-Seventh CPSU Party Congress in February 1986, the first such omission at a Party Congress in thirty years.[13] Worse still, two months later he saw that Soviet naval ships were deliberately withdrawn from Libyan waters two hours before the U.S. airstrikes against Khaddafi.

Despite these disquieting signs, Castro may hope that the Soviets will simply become more selective in exploiting new targets of opportunity in the Third World, particularly where there may be prospects of realizing significant long-term strategic gains against the West (e.g., in the Philippines and southern Africa). Meanwhile, he may be reassured that current Soviet strategy appears intent on consolidating recent investments in the Third World. The Soviets have intensified their efforts to find solutions—if not politically, then militarily—that will protect their equities in Afghanistan, South Yemen, Angola, Ethiopia, and Nicaragua.

Such a consolidative Soviet strategy would dovetail with some of Castro's foreign policy interests. For instance, he is not inclined to let go of his assets in Angola and Nicaragua while he stands to gain as the Soviets escalate their military involvement and material support in Angola. Yet, as discussed below, an enlarged military involvement in Angola could further ensnare Cuba in a protracted, bloody conflict that might not yield the kinds of political, military, and economic payoffs that Castro enjoyed following Cuba's initial intervention in 1975. In Nicaragua, the risks of Cuban military involvement on behalf of the Sandinista regime are even greater.

Equally important, a supportive Cuban role in a Soviet strategy of consolidation is not the kind of role Castro most desires in the Third World. His mindset and behavioral mode have always made him want to achieve new breakthroughs and to lead the way. A consolidative Soviet strategy could cast Cuba in a subservient client role, deprive Castro of his leadership pretensions, and stretch out the calendar for the socialist struggle. In sum, the apparent Soviet deemphasis on the Third World must be frustrating to Cuba's *caudillo*, all the more so because it is in Third World arenas where he has been able to pursue his maximalist ambitions, particularly when he has had Soviet backing, as he did in the post-1975 period.

---

[13]Fukuyama observes, however, that "there is no evidence that the Soviets have cut back on their overall military and economic assistance to the Third World since Brezhnev's death. The economic constraints mentioned in Soviet statements and writings therefore have not yet affected actual behavior, but rather either refer to future policy or, possibly, in the case of economic assistance, constitute a sort of apologia for past performance." (Fukuyama, *Moscow's Post-Brezhnev Reassessment of the Third World*, p. 62.)

A new tougher leadership. These divergencies over the Third World could add to the personal and policy differences that Castro is likely to encounter in dealing with the new Soviet leadership. Even before Gorbachev became General Secretary, Moscow's disinclination to indulge Cuba's economic mismanagement and to fully back its internationalism had prompted Castro to refrain from attending Chernenko's burial and Gorbachev's ascension to power in March 1985.[14] Since then, he has met with the new Soviet Foreign Minister, Eduard Shevardnadze, in an apparent effort to reconcile differences, and he attended the Twenty-Seventh CPSU Party Congress in February 1986, meeting Gorbachev then and later, following his return from North Korea.

Nonetheless, Castro may find that Gorbachev's ascendance and the subsequent leadership changes throughout the Soviet Party and government, could adversely affect his standing with and access to Moscow. With the removal of Grigory Romanov from the Politburo, for example, Castro may have lost a "friend in court," whereas neither Vorotnikov nor Katushev may be his advocate in Moscow. In short, after twenty-six years of dealing with Kremlin leaders, Castro may find that he is confronted with a younger, less familiar and tougher Soviet leadership that could shift the foundations of the Soviet-Cuban relationship from its past ideological, political, and strategic underpinnings to new administrative, institutional, and economic priorities—hardly the Cuban *caudillo's* strengths.

Western Europe: On the Margins of Castro's World View

Western Europe has never loomed as large as the Soviet Union, the United States, the Third World, or Latin America in Castro's mental map of the global struggle. Since the 1960s, the European nations have served as an alternative source for some trade, technology, and financial credit, thus enabling Cuba to compensate a little for the U.S. economic blockade. However, Cuba's economic ties with Western Europe can do little to reduce the island's dependence on the Soviet bloc, given present world market conditions and Cuba's trade commitments with the Soviet Union.

On the political front, Castro has welcomed the increased activism in the Caribbean Basin of the Socialist International (SI) and the Social Democratic parties of Germany and France. Since 1979, these parties have tried to offer political alternatives to resolve U.S.-

---

[14]Castro's excuse was a busy schedule and physical exhaustion; yet soon afterwards he found time to give an extended interview, spanning over three days, to *Playboy* magazine. As a further snub, he reportedly did not deliver the Cuban address during the Soviet embassy's ceremony in Havana honoring Chernenko.

Soviet/Cuban friction over the Nicaraguan revolution. But their actions have also served (if only indirectly) to internationalize the revolutionary conflict in Central America, promote the Contadora process, and put U.S. policy on the defensive, thereby creating minor divisions within the Western alliance. Castro has benefited from all this, but in general, Europe has remained on the margins of his thoughts and actions.

This pattern may persist into the future. At present, however, West European acquiescence to the U.S. intervention in Grenada, growing SI disillusionment over Nicaragua, and European backing of the Duarte government may indicate to Castro that Western Europe is becoming less accommodative of Cuban interests. If so, Europe will provide him with fewer opportunities for helping the Soviets divide the Western alliance and for restraining U.S. policy towards Nicaragua.

In fact, Castro's efforts to expand his communications with European socialist governments have failed where they count most: with Spain's young Socialist leader, Felipe González. After Franco's death, González paid a very friendly visit to Cuba, but as Spain's Prime Minister, he has since become increasingly cool to Castro because of Castro's repressive rule and adventurist behavior. González canceled his scheduled trip to Cuba and Latin America in the summer of 1985, while evading Castro's requests to visit Spain—in marked contrast to the welcome he gave President Reagan in May. Castro has responded by criticizing not only Spanish ties to NATO and the European Community (EC), but also Spain's atrocities during its colonial rule in Cuba. Relations between the two countries took a turn for the worse when Cuban embassy officials tried to kidnap a defecting colleague in Madrid in December 1985; they were thwarted and expelled from Spain. The affair ended in an angry exchange of diplomatic notes between the two governments.[15]

The greatest potential costs and benefits for Castro in dealing with European governments may result from European security perceptions about Cuba and Nicaragua. The European members of NATO have not subscribed to the U.S. view that the military capabilities growing in Cuba represent a potential wartime threat to NATO supply lines passing between Florida and Cuba, nor more generally, do they agree that the expansion of a Cuban-Nicaraguan military axis would divert U.S. military attention and resources from Europe toward protecting the southern approaches to the U.S. mainland. A fundamental shift

---

[15]For an analysis of the strained Spanish-Cuban relationship, including the defection incident, see Edward Schumacher, "Disagreeing, but in a Common Tongue," *The New York Times*, December 22, 1985, p. IV-E3.

among European political and military leaders toward either of these views might be costly to Castro's interests.

Meanwhile, events in Grenada and Nicaragua have caused European views to move somewhat more in line with U.S. views than was the case a few years ago. The best that Castro may hope for is that Western Europe will remain a factor helping to constrain the United States from pursuing direct military measures against Cuba or Nicaragua.

THE NORTH-SOUTH STRUGGLE: DECLINING OPPORTUNITIES, NEW COMPLEXITIES

Things are not going so well for Castro in Third World arenas either. He is proud of the revolutionary advances in Angola and Nicaragua. He still has hopes for further breakthroughs elsewhere. And he can still use political extortion to pressure specific Latin American governments. But as a whole, current trends in the Third World and the North-South struggle present new complexities that are not to his liking:

- Potential opportunities loom in southern Africa, but Cuba may also be tied down in a costly war in Angola.
- Prospects for revolution are receding in Central America.
- The U.S.-led intervention in Grenada and the recent ouster of the Duvalier regime from Haiti have strengthened U.S. influence in the Caribbean Basin.
- Opportunities for exploiting the Latin American debt crisis are offset by the renewal of the region's democratic tendencies and overriding interests in good economic relations with the West.
- The Non-Aligned Movement and the militant campaign for a "new international economic order" have declined in importance as anti-U.S. and anti-imperialist vehicles.
- The newly industrializing capitalist-oriented countries of Southeast Asia provide successful performance models that stand in contrast to Cuba and other struggling socialist economies.
- Other militantly anti-American countries, notably Libya and Iran, have taken to playing on the world stage in recent years; but far from being willing allies of Cuba, they have acted partly as competitors.

For Castro, these trends are especially disturbing because they are taking place precisely in the theaters where he traditionally has had great influence and success.

Opportunities and Growing Risks in Southern Africa

In South Africa, growing internal violence and international reaction against the Botha government may enable Cuba to gain new political capital in the Third World by championing the cause of the antiapartheid forces. The South African situation may even present him with the justification for expanding Cuba's military presence in southern Africa, although such a venture would face both substantial obstacles and risks.

Castro may hope that a further deterioration in South Africa's situation could weaken Pretoria's commitment to Angola's National Union for the Total Independence of Angola (UNITA), led by Jonas Savimbi. Thus far, Savimbi's guerrilla forces control the countryside in the southeastern quadrant of Angola. If South Africa were to disengage, the Cuban and Soviet-backed forces of the Popular Movement for the Liberation of Angola (MPLA) could eventually gain the upper hand in the Angolan civil war, which has lasted for more than a decade.

In Angola, however, the military outlook may not be reassuring for Castro, judging from recent developments. The survival of the MPLA government still depends on the presence of 30,000 Cuban combat troops, as well as the Soviet and Cuban military advisers who direct and train MPLA forces and operate sophisticated heavy weapons. Despite the infusion of those weapons, MPLA forces have been unable to defeat UNITA. In fact, after launching a major Soviet-directed offensive in July and August 1985, the MPLA forces were badly mauled by the South African-supported UNITA counteroffensive in September, forcing the withdrawal of MPLA forces at Mavinga. Further large-scale encounters probably will have to await the return of the dry season in summer 1986.

By then, however, UNITA will have begun receiving U.S. military assistance, including the first shipments of shoulder-fired Stinger antiaircraft missiles that can be used against Soviet MiG jet fighters and MI-24 Hind helicopter gunships.[16] A stronger insurgency could strengthen the hand of moderate elements within the MPLA who have advocated an accommodation with Savimbi and UNITA. To block

---

[16] According to U.S. sources, the first shipment of 50 Stinger missiles arrived in April 1986, together with U.S. advisers; the Soviets reportedly countered by adding three squadrons of MI-25 helicopters and two squadrons of MI-24 helicopters. (*The Washington Times*, April 21, 1986, p. 5.)

such a development, and also defeat UNITA, Havana and Moscow might therefore increase Cuba's military role in Angola to support hardline elements in the MPLA.

For its part, the Soviet Union appears committed to assuring the survival of a Marxist-Leninist regime in Luanda,[17] if necessary, through a military solution. Since mid-1983, the Soviets have supplied MiG-21 jet fighters, tanks and armored personnel carriers, and SA-8 missiles for air defense against South African aircraft. Since early 1984, these arms transfers have been augmented by MiG-23 Flogger and SU-22 Fitter jet aircraft and MI-24 Hind helicopter gunships, manned by Cuban and Soviet personnel. In addition, the Soviets evidently have begun providing maintenance service and strategic guidance and coordination as they did in Ethiopia. There are some indications that the Soviets have also become involved in direct military training and combat activities.[18]

The escalation of the Soviet commitment to Angola holds both potential advantages and risks for Castro. He could gain renewed leverage with Moscow, as he did after 1975, because Cuban combat forces are needed to ensure the defeat of UNITA.[19] However, if the war in Angola should escalate, he could face new risks greater than any since Cuba's initial military intervention in 1975:

- Cuban troops already face a stronger adversary in UNITA, and there may be far more Cuban casualties than there were a decade ago. The certainty of being bloodied will increase substantially if the South Africans are drawn into the war.
- With the repeal of the Clark Amendment, Washington no longer would be prohibited, as it was after 1975, from rendering additional assistance to the anti-Communist insurgency in Angola.
- Cuba's civilian population and military circles appear less willing to support an escalated war effort in distant Angola, particularly if casualties are high, as indicated by civilian opposition to military service, the behavior of Colonel Tortoló Comás

---

[17]The following information is based on research being conducted by Alexander R. Alexiev and Nanette C. Brown of The Rand Corporation.

[18]Thus, *Izvestiya*, March 23, 1985, extolled Soviet "specialists" who "live in battlefield conditions" and "work under fire."

[19]In March 1985, prior to the summer offensive, Cuba was called into high-level "consultations" in Moscow on the Angolan issue. Among those attending the meeting were Soviet Foreign Minister Andre Gromyko; Boris Ponomarev, Chief of the International Department of the Central Committee of the CPSU; and Jorge Risquet, a member of the PCC Political Bureau, who is in charge of Cuba's Angolan policy. (See *Pravda*, March 8, 1985.)

and his staff, and the defection of Lieutenant Colonel Joaquín Mouriño Pérez.
- Heightened Cuban participation in a Soviet-directed Angolan war could further discredit Cuba as a Soviet proxy among many Third World regimes, as occurred with Cuba's involvement in Ethiopia in 1977–78.
- If Cuban involvement escalates in Angola, Castro would not have the initiative in dealing with Moscow as he evidently did in the 1975 intervention, but would be responding to Soviet demands and Angolan developments.

Still, Castro's risk assessment may not discourage him from increasing Cuba's stakes in Angola. As discussed earlier, his hubris-nemesis complex virtually compels him to try to defeat the United States and thereby revalidate his destiny. Indeed, in May 1985, he publicly vowed to send more troops to Angola as needed to match any U.S.-backed escalation of the war.

The Ebbing of the Revolutionary Tide in Central America

In Nicaragua, the Sandinista regime faces a critical period in the coming years during which it must defeat the Contras while also discouraging direct U.S. military action. The presence of 2,000 to 3,000 Cuban military advisers, until recently headed by Division General Arnaldo T. Ochoa,[20] and the increased arms transfers by the Soviet Union, including the MI-24 Hind helicopter gunship, give the 60,000-man Sandinista army the military advantage at the present time. The regime's extensive political controls also enable it to mobilize segments of the population and intimidate the political opposition, as evidenced by the October 1985 decree suspending civil rights.

Nevertheless, Castro must be concerned over the prospects for survival of his client regime in Nicaragua and the extent to which Cuba's own security might be endangered by Nicaraguan developments. As sympathy for the Sandinista regime erodes in the U.S. Congress, the Reagan administration may eventually secure passage of $70 million in military aid as well as some $30 million in humanitarian assistance for the Contras. Such a measure could become the first step in building up the insurgent forces to 25,000 men or more. An expanded, well-trained Contra army supplied with modern weapons to neutralize San-

---

[20]On March 11, 1986, Brigadier General Nestor López Cuba replaced Ochoa as Cuba's Military Adviser in Nicaragua. Ochoa enjoyed considerable stature as a result of his success in commanding Cuban combat forces in Ethiopia during the 1977–78 war with Somalia.

dinista firepower and the MI-24 helicopters could create serious military and political problems for the FSLN regime in the not-too-distant future.

The Sandinista regime already faces growing popular discontent over the worsening economic and political situation. At the very least, the news of Contra victories could rally the anti-Communist opposition forces in the Church, the private sector, and political parties. Worse yet for hardline elements within the regime, moderate elements might begin pushing for some kind of accommodation with the political and military opposition. More direct Cuban involvement might then seem the only way to prevent the unraveling of the Sandinista regime—but such a development would risk U.S. military retaliation against Cuba and Nicaragua.[21]

Although it is not likely in the near term, Castro must also be concerned that the Reagan administration might ultimately deploy U.S. air and naval power to support the Contra army once it gains a strong combat position on the battlefield. In this scenario, Cuba would be faced with the difficult choice of either forgoing its client or opposing the United States in a military showdown in Nicaragua, with the prospect of the war engulfing Cuba itself—a prospect that Castro avoided in Grenada by not aiding the Cuban resistance on the island. Even if Cuba did not aid Nicaragua, there is still a possibility that the United States would carry out preemptive airstrikes against the Cuban air force to ensure the security of the Caribbean sea lanes during a Nicaraguan intervention.

In El Salvador, the insurgency appears stalemated, with the prospects of the FMLN emerging victorious now fading. Since 1984, military trends have favored the U.S.-backed Duarte government: The FMLN has not been able to carry out a dry-season offensive against the increasingly better led, motivated, and trained Salvadoran army. The FMLN has also found it more and more difficult to recruit new combatants from the civilian population. Faced with the growing firepower of government forces, the FMLN has had to rely on terrorism and small-unit operations in what it now concedes will be a protracted, decades-long war.[22]

Political trends are also running against the FMLN: Napoleon Duarte's election in 1984 gave the Salvadoran government a domestic and international legitimacy that was previously lacking, enabling Washington to increase its military and economic support. The major

---

[21]Momentary defeat of the Contras would also be risky for Cuba because the United States might then decide to intervene militarily to dislodge the Sandinista regime.

[22]See *The New York Times*, December 22, 1985, pp. 1, 8.

bright spot for the FMLN is that Duarte's internal image has suffered as a result of his handling of his daughter's kidnapping last fall, while public reaction against the government has increased with the implementation of new economic austerity measures. Indeed, because of the structural problems facing El Salvador, there remains a long-term potential for a violent Marxist-led revolution. At present, however, the short- to medium-term prospects have receded.

Immediate trends are also not favorable to Castro in Guatemala, Honduras, or Costa Rica, in contrast to the revolutionary expectations of the early 1980s. The Guatemalan insurgency remains truncated because of the effectiveness of the military's counterinsurgency operations. The assumption of power by President Marco Vinicio Cerezo Arevalo in January 1986, the first democratically elected civilian head of government in Guatemala since 1966, will facilitate the resumption of needed U.S. economic and security assistance. Meanwhile, the democratic regime of Costa Rica is mired in economic difficulties, but Washington is providing economic aid and, for the first time, military assistance to improve the proficiency of the Costa Rican Civil Guard. In neither Costa Rica nor Honduras, whose military has also been strengthened by U.S. assistance, are there prospects for revolutionary upheaval.

Over the longer term, Castro may believe that the revolutionary tide could again begin to sweep over other societies in and outside the Central America region, including Chile, post-Duvalier Haiti, the Dominican Republic, and Puerto Rico, where political instability and troubled economies could open up opportunities for renewed Cuban involvement. For the present, however, these possibilities remain downstream as well as problematic.

Opportunities for Political Extortion

As the prospects for immediate revolution decline, Castro may shift his focus to opportunities for extortion, especially against Honduras and Costa Rica, and possibly Panama and Mexico. In Central America, the governments of Costa Rica and Honduras are fearful of Cuban and Nicaraguan support for revolutionary subversion. They are also apprehensive that the United States might cut a separate deal with Nicaragua and Cuba, and/or abandon them altogether in future years, thereby leaving them to face Nicaragua and the revolutionary threat on their own.

From Castro's vantage point, Honduras may appear particularly vulnerable to extortion—as well as deserving of his vindictiveness—because of its collaboration with the United States in allowing Honduran territory to be used for Contra training camps and staging bases. Cuba trained and supported a small guerrilla group that invaded Honduras from Nicaragua in 1983. Doomed from the outset, the invasion may nevertheless have been intended to serve as a warning to elements of the Honduran government of what Cuba could do. Moreover, the large U.S. presence in Honduras may enable Castro to play on the Honduran fear of U.S. abandonment to motivate the Hondurans to consider cutting their own deal with Nicaragua.[23]

Castro may also be looking at Panama, a country beset by mounting economic problems, social unrest, and heavy-handedness and corruption among the National Guard under the command of General Manuel Antonio Noriega.[24] Together with recurrent nationalist reaction over the remaining U.S. military presence in the Canal Zone, these problems may provide Castro with issues to exploit in his attempts to pressure the Noriega regime to change its policies toward both Havana and Washington. In fact, the Cuban leader may see certain parallels between Panama and the Philippines: In the presence of growing political ferment, Castro would like to stir up troubles that could lead to the removal of the U.S. military presence that has existed in each country since the turn of the century. But unlike the Philippines, Panama is within easy reach of his subversive efforts, including via the Cuban trading companies on the isthmus.

Castro might someday be tempted to pursue his maximalist ambitions by contributing to a destabilization of Mexico, if its political system ever begins to collapse—a possibility that does not appear likely.[25] Barring such developments, Castro seems more likely to try to use political extortion or convivial diplomatic maneuvering to try to influence Mexico to oppose U.S. foreign policy on selected issues. Castro may calculate that Mexico's political fragility, combined with the pro-Castro sympathies of some elements of the Mexican elite, mean that Mexico City must preserve good relations with Havana if the ruling Institutional Revolutionary Party (PRI) is to continue successfully managing the Mexican left.

---

[23]In earlier decades the growth of U.S. involvement in a small country like Honduras would have created primarily a fear of potential U.S. domination and exploitation. But Vietnam and policy shifts from one U.S. administration to the next have eroded local faith in many nations about the reliability and durability of U.S. involvements. Hence, in a country like Honduras, the new fear of eventual U.S. abandonment may now be stronger than the traditional fear of U.S. domination—and Castro knows how to exploit this.

[24]Recent violent confrontations between student and labor forces, the IMF-approved austerity program, and open accusations against Noriega about drug smuggling and intelligence dealings with Cuba could lead to a new spiral of opposition violence.

[25]On factors affecting Mexico's stability, see Ronfeldt, *The Modern Mexican Military*.

Latin America: Debt and Democracy

Latin America's *worsening debt problem* has given Castro a potent issue to exploit against the United States and in favor of Latin Americanism. This was much in evidence during the summer and fall 1985 meetings held in Havana, including a much publicized conference of Latin American delegates that was convened at the end of July on the debt issue. Castro's calls for a cancellation of the Latin American debt, or a strike by the debtor countries in repaying interest and principal, and his harangues against the "greedy" and "selfish" Western world, have appealed to some Latin Americans and put pressure on their governments.

Thus far, however, Argentina, Brazil, Colombia, Mexico, Peru, and other states have not followed Castro's lead. On the contrary, in an interview published in *Le Monde*, Peruvian President Alan García sharply repudiated Castro's call for a Latin American debt strike and his pretensions to lead the Latin American struggle:

> I have great respect for Fidel Castro. At one point in history Cuba represented a very important departure. But when you claim to be a revolutionary the essential thing is to suffer the consequences of the decisions or wishes you express. . . . Our position is realistic. We are part of the interdependent world. *Those who advocate total refusal to repay the debt have a childish, unrealistic, and extremist attitude* [emphasis added].[26]

In fact, Castro had already been feuding with García prior to the *Le Monde* interview, not only over García's position on the debt issue but also over his commitment to reform and anti-imperialism.[27] Perhaps part of Castro's resentment stems from the fact that the Peruvian leader is 22 years younger than he, and, as a social democrat and leader of the American Popular Revolutionary Alliance (APRA), is unwilling to recognize Castro's leadership of the Latin American left.

García's position reflects the problem Castro now faces with the *resurgence of moderate, democratic civilian regimes* in several Latin American countries that were previously under military rule, and the strengthening of the democratic process in others that were already

---

[26]*Le Monde*, September 25, 1985.

[27]In an earlier message to the 36-year-old recently elected Peruvian President, Castro described Peru as a country having "social inequality and misery of all kinds," adding that "if you decide to fight seriously, firmly and consistently against this Dantesque panorama of social calamities, and to liberate your country as you have promised from the domination of and dependence on imperialism, which is the only cause of this tragedy, you can count on Cuba's support." García replied by declaring, "I answer to the people of Peru and not to any foreign ruler in carrying out what I have promised." (*The New York Times*, September 15, 1985, p. 4.)

under civilian rule. Although they may be faced with indigenous or Cuban-backed Marxist insurgencies, democratic governments in Colombia, Peru, and Venezuela are not likely to fall. Meanwhile, they, along with the Argentine and Brazilian governments, see the economic interests of their countries as tied to the industrialized West rather than the Third World or Cuba and the Soviet bloc. Such countries are thus not likely to fall in step with Castro's campaign for two Americas, in which Latin America would form an entity that excludes the United States. Worse still, from the *líder máximo's* viewpoint, they may exploit his radical stance to their own bargaining advantage in dealing with Washington and others in the Western world.

A More Fractious, Less Militant Third World

The Third World of the 1980s is evolving in patterns that defy Castro's earlier expectations. He must be concerned about the emergence of *charismatic rivals and Islamic fundamentalism* in the Middle East. In the recent past, the PLO, which has collaborated with Cuba and Nicaragua, exemplified Arab radicalism and anti-Americanism. Now, however, the charismatic appeal of the Ayatollah Khomeini and the anti-Westernism of his Iranian revolution present problems because Castro's Marxism-Leninism cannot be reconciled with Islamic fundamentalism. Similarly, the charismatic presence and grand ambitions of Mohamar Khaddafi have made strategic (as opposed to tactical) collaboration between Cuba and the Arab world virtually impossible. Indeed, Khaddafi is himself a rival for leadership of the Third World and the Non-Aligned Movement.

Elsewhere, the *newly industrializing countries* (NICs) of Asia are serving as examples for the rest of the Third World. As market- and export-oriented economies that are closely integrated into the capitalist global economy, the NICs have succeeded in establishing a growth momentum that other Third World states are now trying to emulate. In turn, more and more Third World states are abandoning, to Castro's chagrin, the militant, multilateral approach that demanded a "new international economic order" in favor of bilateral economic ties to the West. Hence, many of the Third World countries attending the World Bank meeting in Seoul in October 1985 supported the new American debt strategy designed to pump an additional $30 billion over three years into those Third World countries that apply market-oriented policies to increase domestic savings, investments, and growth.

Castro may increasingly fear that the Third World is eluding his grasp as his principal theater of operation and influence. He now has rivals, both contending charismatic leaders and ideologies. Major

Third World players are becoming less militant and more accommodative toward the West, as exemplified by India after Indira Gandhi. The Non-Aligned Movement is likely to become more divided and less effective as an anti-U.S. forum. Castro faces the prospects of becoming increasingly isolated from a new generation of political and intellectual leadership, exemplified by Alan García and Rajiv Gandhi.

NEW FORCES ENTERING CASTRO'S WORLD VIEW

Castro surely is most concerned with the domestic and international problems discussed above. Even so, it must be remembered that he constantly seeks to grasp new ideas and technologies that may profoundly affect Cuba's and mankind's future. Thus he has been quietly showing a steadily increasing interest in two powerful new forces, both of which are difficult to reconcile with traditional Marxist thinking:

- The growth of the "information revolution" worldwide, and the spread of new computer and communication technologies.
- The growth of "liberation theology" in the Catholic Church, and its implications for legitimizing revolutionary change in Latin America.

The Information Revolution: A Long-Range Interest?

By many accounts, the "information revolution" will succeed the industrial revolution as the next great stage in man's history. Through the spread of new computer, communication, and robotic technologies, the information revolution has already begun to change the ways in which governments, the military, private corporations, and revolutionary and terrorist organizations as well, conduct their affairs.[28]

Will this matter much to Cuba? Little is known about Castro's views on this issue, but he seems to have a nascent interest in the information revolution. He became a master at using television for mass communication and international projection as early as 1959. In 1963, at his "persistent and personal urging," Cuba acquired its first computer, a British model called the "Elliot."[29] In 1969, the Political

---

[28]See Jean-Paul Emard, *Information and Telecommunications: An Overview of Issues, Technologies, and Applications*, Washington, D.C.: Science Policy Research Division, Congressional Research Service, Library of Congress, 1981; Geza Feketekuty and Jonathan D. Aronson, "Meeting the Challenges of the World Information Economy," *The World Economy*, Vol. 3, No. 84, pp. 63-86.

[29]According to Osvaldo Dorticós, "Desarrollar cultural, scientifica, y tecnicamente los cuadros administrativos," *Economía y Desarrollo*, November-December 1973, pp. 26-57.

Bureau of the Cuban Communist Party began authorizing the introduction of computers for economic planning and management, and this objective was written into the platform of the 1975 Party Congress. Meanwhile in the 1970s, Castro directed some offices in his government to experiment with computers for accounting and planning purposes, and a few university training centers were established.[30] In 1978, the Computer Training Center of the National Institute of Automated Systems and Computer Techniques (INSAC) was created, and working relations were established with similar Soviet-bloc organizations.[31] At the same time, Cuba acquired dozens of additional computers, and Castro inspired a domestic effort to construct some models—known as CID models, apparently named after the Centro de Investigación Digital at the University of Havana—using Soviet bloc technology and assistance.[32]

Now, in the mid-1980s, Cuba is building a later generation of elementary minicomputers (e.g., the CID 300/10 model). Cuba exports some components to the Soviet bloc and continues to acquire computers and related hardware and software, including U.S. (IBM) and Japanese (NEC and Sanyo) products, via Panama and other countries. INSAC trains foreign students as well as Cubans. The Ministry of Public Health and the Institute of Marketing have the largest facilities and staffs using computers for planning and accounting purposes. According to Castro's speech at the Third Party Congress, the electronics industry and computerization will be among the top priorities in the upcoming phase of Cuba's development. Steps have been taken "to include computer techniques in education, public health, scientific investigation, transportation, and production processes." In addition to producing microcomputers, Cuba will further develop the production of certain components and semiconductors. And the Cuban military has

---

Dorticós highlights the importance of this purchase by claiming (pp. 29-31) that the United States tried to block Cuba from getting computers as though they were as important as atomic missiles. This article is a reprint of a speech by Dorticós inaugurating the Instituto de Informatica at the Central University (Las Villas).

[30] For example, the Instituto de Informatica at the Central University (Las Villas), and the Centro de Informatica Aplicada a la Gestion (CINAG) at the University of Havana. Pedro Pablo Villanueva, "Algunas cuestiones sobre la determinacion de la efectividad economica del subsistema: dirección del abastecimiento tecnico-material," *Economía y Desarrollo*, July-August, 1978, pp. 46-49, points out (p. 48) that "in the present stage of the construction of the socialist society in our country, the application of electronic computers ... may be considered experimental and investigatory in nature."

[31] "'Modern technology' used at computer training center," *Granma Weekly Review*, April 21, 1985, p. 5.

[32] Dorticós, "Desarrolar cultural, ..." 1973, p. 51.

taken some steps toward using computer techniques to automate the command procedures of some staffs, and to improve the nation's early warning system.[33]

Finally, Castro keeps in a small room next to his office some IBM microcomputers that one observer has described as "the brain of the Cuban government."[34] Castro has reportedly programmed one personal computer with Latin American bank debt data so that he can regale visitors with algorithmic forecasts of impending doom.[35]

Cuba has thus slowly acquired practical technical capabilities in this area. It is far from being a leader at "informatics" or "telematics" in Latin America or the Third World, partly because the U.S. economic blockade has circumscribed access to the best technology and training, but also because the Soviet Union lags behind in this area.[36] Despite such constraints, Cuba's capabilities and motivations are growing, and Castro has taken a personal interest.

In the years ahead, Cuba may try to take advantage of the information revolution (1) by developing the required technical capabilities for use at home and abroad, and (2) by exploiting, in the Cuban-Soviet relationship as well as in international and regional arenas, the data flows and policy issues that emerge. The possibilities may include the following:

- The Soviets maintain an important electronic intelligence facility in Cuba that collects information from the United States. If the use of Cuban troops abroad declines as a measure of Cuba's importance to the Soviet Union, this facility (not to mention the Soviet Union's other fixed assets in Cuba, e.g., the military facilities) may become relatively more important as a stake in Cuban-Soviet bargaining relations.
- Cuba might aim to become a low-cost center for some electronic assembly and database input work for the Soviet bloc, emulating the offshore roles that Singapore and Taiwan have begun to play for U.S.-based corporations that face high labor costs at home. For example, at a Council for Economic Mutual Advantage (CEMA) meeting in 1985, Carlos Rafael Rodríguez report-

---

[33]From the report on Castro's speech in *FBIS*, February 7, 1986, pp. Q16, Q24, Q30.

[34]*Fidel e a Religiao: Conversas com Frei Betto*. Friar Betto's description refers only to census-type data, however.

[35]See the brief discussion in Sec. II of Castro's use of econometric and mathematical formulas for analyzing debt data.

[36]The Soviet Union lags not only for technological reasons, but also because the Soviet leadership did not begin resolving until the mid-1960s its blocwide debate about how to make cybernetics consistent with Marxism-Leninism.

edly proposed that Cuba be allowed to specialize in electronics. (The proposal was not approved.)[37]
- Over time, the information revolution may result in the creation of, and the need for, a new generation of technocratic ("cybercratic") elites in Cuba who are skilled in applying the new technologies and want to influence economic planning, administration, and policy.[38]
- The new technologies may enhance Cuba's capability to communicate quickly with revolutionary groups in other countries; exchange information with them; exercise central coordination, command, and control functions; and affect tactical decisions.
- Cuba may tap into data banks and information flows available via satellites in Cuba's vicinity (e.g., the Galaxy satellite over Mexico, and others over the United States).
- More generally, the information revolution may give rise to a range of sensitive international policy issues that Cuba can exploit.

This last point may prove attractive to Castro. There are no available data on Cuban positions on information issues raised in such international bodies as UNESCO, the Non-Aligned Movement (NAM), the Intergovernmental Bureau of Informatics (IBI), and the International Telecommunications Union (ITU). However, Cuban positions on information revolution issues resemble Soviet positions, emphasizing themes such as "information sovereignty" and "information imperialism." Cuba subscribes to the Soviet view that the socialist system is better suited than the capitalist system to benefit from the information revolution. Proponents of this view hold that the information revolution will ultimately aggravate the capitalist system's tendencies toward unemployment and overproduction.

This pattern emerged during the late 1970s and early 1980s when Cuba joined other Soviet bloc, NAM, and Third World nations in developing the movement for a "new world information order" that emanated from UNESCO and resulted in a narrow effort to impose standards for the state regulation of journalists and their reportage, particularly on the Western news services. This movement has since

---

[37]The recent appointment of Ramiro Valdés to a leadership post in Cuba's electronics sector, following his removal as Minister of Interior, may be an indicator of the growing importance of the intelligence, industrial, and administrative applications of the computer revolution.

[38]Though the issue is not discussed here, a full-scale adoption of the new technology, particularly personal computers, would surely raise questions about economic planning and political decentralization that might not be to Castro's liking.

abated, and Castro is far more interested in sustaining the earlier, broader call for a "new international economic order."

Looking ahead, the technologies of the information revolution will gradually give rise to a distinctive, new generation of North-South and East-West issues, including access to international data banks, the regulation of transborder data flows, the propagation of direct broadcast satellites, and cable television systems. Some of these will probably attract Castro's and Cuba's attention, although it is difficult to forecast which ones, and when.[39]

In sum, the information revolution may offer few issues of immediate opportunity for Castro, and Cuba cannot claim to be an information-technology leader among Latin American or Third World nations. But the rapidly growing importance of the information revolution, Castro's apparent interest in it, and the fact that it raises sensitive North-South and East-West issues may mean that close attention to informatics in Cuba is warranted.

Religion and Revolution: Fidel the Liberation Theologist

While informatics remains a nascent interest, Castro is showing a sudden strong interest in religion. Rapid religious change is sweeping much of the world, cutting deeply into political life where it occurs and promising to be one of the most dynamic forces of the late twentieth century. Some of the new religious forces pose a direct challenge to Marxism. But others offer Marxists growing opportunities to:

- Enlist new allies among radical priests and their communities.
- Foment divisions in both the Catholic and Protestant churches, particularly in Latin America and the United States.
- Use religious institutions as vehicles for opposing or supporting particular governments.

Why is Castro interested in religious issues now? The reasons are varied. Castro needs to control and get ahead of the revival of religious sentiments and organization within Cuba, which could weaken his regime's ideological legitimacy and system of social control. He may also want to appeal to the growing international audience of radical Catholics. Yet it should be recalled that Castro responds most strongly when he takes things personally. He dislikes criticism and opposition

---

[39]Castro's recent intemperate reaction to the startup of Radio Martí reflects his sensitivity to information-related issues. For some general background on potential future issues, see David Webster, "Direct Broadcast Satellites: Proximity, Sovereignty, and National Identity," *Foreign Affairs*, Summer 1984, pp. 1161–1174, and "Toward a New World Information Order?" *Journal of International Affairs*, Special Issue, Fall/Winter 1981/2.

from any quarter. He competes with any new leaders who may be potential rivals. And he seizes opportunities that enable him to express his ideals and create difficulties for his rivals and enemies. These personal traits may help explain his sudden interest in religion: He may want to upstage or counter the Pope.

Pope John Paul II has pursued conservative, visibly anti-Communist policies. He has cautiously worked to restrain liberation theology priests from adopting Marxist viewpoints and advocating violent change. In so doing, he has had a strong impact in Latin America, which he has visited four times. While visiting Nicaragua in 1983, he pointedly rebuked the Sandinista priest turned government official, Ernesto Cardenal. And he has steadfastly supported Managua-based Cardinal Miguel Obando y Bravo, who is a strong and popular critic of Sandinista policies, and a leading light of moderate opposition forces in Nicaragua.

All of this is contrary to Castro's designs. He may not conceive of himself as a revolutionary nemesis of the Pope in Latin America, but he is certainly aroused sufficiently to begin pontificating about his own views of religion.

He made a few statements about religion during the 1970s, notably while visiting Chile in 1971 and Jamaica in 1977. He recently issued a major dramatic statement in *Fidel e a Religiao: Conversas com Frei Betto (Fidel and Religion: Conversations with Friar Betto)*. The book was published in Brazil and Cuba in November 1985 and has since sold 800,000 copies in Cuba alone. Meanwhile, Castro has been meeting frequently with visiting religious leaders from Latin America, Western Europe, and the United States. He has been making overtures toward improved relations between Cuba and the Vatican, and he has been angling for the Pope to visit Cuba. Within Cuba, he met with Catholic bishops twice during 1985 in what has been touted as a "dialogue" that could lead to a reconciliation between Church and state. This could provide more religious freedom for the former and a needed patina of respectability for the latter among practicing Catholics.[40]

Castro has used his early religious training in Jesuit schools[41] to support his claim that he is more qualified to talk about religion than were visiting U.S. bishops to talk about revolution:

---

[40]In related activities, a new Office of Religious Affairs has been attached to the PCC Central Committee. As for the Church's position within Cuba, opposition to discrimination against religious believers was voiced at the Third Party Congress. Catholics are still barred from the Party, although improvements in Church-state relations may well occur in the future as a result of Castro's efforts to woo Church support. For background, see Margaret E. Crahan, "Cuba: Religion and Revolutionary Institutionalization," *Journal of Latin American Studies*, November 1983, pp. 319–340.

[41]See Secs. II and III for details.

I said to the bishops that we would talk with no reservations, no biases of any kind, that we were looking to communicating differing viewpoints. I did say that, in my opinion, I was in better condition to talk in that spirit since I had attended religious schools from the first grade up to my last senior year in high school. I had, moreover, lived the whole experience of religion, of the Church, of religious work; but none of them had attended a Party school. That's the difference.[42]

The central theme Castro may develop is his view of the compatibility of Marxism and Christianity, particularly as expressed in the tendency of liberation theology to legitimize revolutionary change on behalf of the poor. This would fit with his image of himself as a principled, moral crusader, and it would take strategic advantage of the growth of radical religious forces and the increasing vulnerability of politics and governments to religious forces.[43] In addition, religion offers him a new tactical instrument that, in the current environment, may be less risky but just as effective as the political and military instruments he is accustomed to using.

By exploiting schisms and fomenting polarization within the Catholic Church, Castro may seek to assume *de facto* leadership of the radical clergy and the liberation theology movement, undermine the Church's traditional institutional strength, and challenge the role of the Church hierarchy, including the Pope, in Latin America. Of greater political significance, he may seek to forge a broad coalition, if not a united front, of revolutionary Marxists and radical Catholics under Havana's auspices. Whether he plays a clear or a cloaked leadership role, he could use an instrument such as religion, in some situations, to embarrass, weaken, and isolate a government and to moralize revolutionary violence against it (e.g., in Chile or South Africa); in other situations, he could use it to rally support for a favored government (e.g., Nicaragua) or issue (e.g., the debt).[44] In addition, religious activism by Castro might appeal to leftist proponents of the sanctuary movement in the United States, who oppose U.S. policy in Central America.

Castro does face problems in seeking to exploit religion, not the least of which is the formidable institution he faces in the Catholic Church. Despite his claims to having received religious training as a child, his

---

[42]Castro, *Granma Weekly Review*, February 24, 1985, p. 6.

[43]Castro has periodically called for a strategic alliance between religion and socialism, between religion and revolution, since his trip to Chile in 1971. (See *Fidel e a Religiao: Conversas com Frei Betto.*)

[44]Castro has not gone so far as to propose a formal regionwide organization, but a precedent exists in the Havana-based Latin American Solidarity Organization (OLAS) of the middle to late 1960s.

leadership over a Marxist-Catholic coalition would surely be suspect.[45] It would be difficult to reconcile with his role as the First Secretary of the Communist Party in Cuba and with the heightened repression of the Church in Nicaragua, which, after all, is a client of Cuba. Such contradictions should limit the viability of a coalition among radicalized Catholics and Marxist-Leninists.

In sum, a religious gambit may not yield major revolutionary returns for Castro in Latin America. But it could be divisive and might provide him with yet another means for political extortion against established governments and the Church hierarchy. It might also be personally gratifying to Castro to venture into the realm of religion at a time when he faces so many obstacles in the areas of politics and economics. South Africa might provide a more susceptible environment than Latin America for such a gambit.

CASTRO'S LEADERSHIP IMAGE PROBLEM: THE NEED TO TRIUMPH ANEW

The constraints on Cuba and the closing of opportunities on the international front have made it increasingly difficult for Castro to project an image of statesmanship and strong, successful leadership. Until recently, his past accomplishments and his ability to escape responsibility for major policy errors by directly or indirectly blaming others have enabled him to sustain his image.[46] In October 1983, however, Grenada became a strategic foreign policy defeat, perhaps equivalent to the harvest debacle of 1970. Since Grenada, Castro has not had a major breakthrough either at home or abroad with which to recover his leadership image. Worse yet, he has sometimes shown himself to be irrational and erratic in his recent policies.

Grenada: Miscalculation and Failure

In Grenada, Cuba lost not only a close revolutionary ally but also some of its credibility as a world-class actor. Grenada demonstrated the powerlessness of Cuba and the readiness of the Soviets to abandon clients in the region in the face of U.S. armed might. Moreover, as with the harvest failure, Grenada revealed serious flaws in Castro's

---

[45]When pressed about contradictions between Marxism and Christianity, Castro tends to emphasize that he is a follower of Martí's ideas, which he says are entirely compatible with Christianity.

[46]His acknowledgment of his role in the 1970 harvest failure was the major exception, and it weakened his authority and opened the way for a more Soviet-style order.

leadership ability. He has maintained that he and his government were unaware of the extent to which Maurice Bishop was being opposed and outmaneuvered by the Bernard Coard faction on Grenada.[47] This is in itself an extraordinary admission of personal as well as governmental incompetence: Not only was the Cuban ambassador in daily contact with Bishop, the Grenadian leader was Castro's protégé and had visited him in Havana only days prior to the coup. Hence, Castro could not escape responsibility for Cuba's intelligence failure in Grenada.

Like the 1962 missile crisis, Grenada also revealed Castro's willingness to put Cuba at risk in his confrontation with the United States. By ordering Cuban contingents on Grenada to resist and not surrender, he may have hoped that the resulting U.S. casualties would turn American public opinion against the Reagan administration and constrain it from invading Nicaragua. If so, he put Cuba on a direct collision course with the United States. He also seriously overestimated the extent to which Cuban construction workers, and especially the small contingent of Cuban military personnel, would be willing to sacrifice themselves for a higher international cause. Among Cuba's younger, better educated and more technically competent generation of civilian and military leaders, many of whom do not share the guerrilla veterans' personal loyalty and veneration toward their leader, Grenada may have appeared both dangerous and irrational, eroding their confidence in Castro's leadership abilities.

Post-Grenada: Erratic Policy Behavior

Castro's leadership image problem may have been further compounded by his subsequent flip-flops in Cuban domestic priorities and in his policy toward the United States. At the height of the people's war campaign, Castro suddenly announced the signing of a new migration agreement with Washington in December 1984. Addressing the Cuban people on television, he explained that the agreement, together with U.S. government efforts to curb Cuban exile activities, heralded a significant change in U.S.-Cuban policy, despite the known hostility of the Reagan administration toward the Castro regime.[48] Priorities were shifted as Castro declared war on Cuba's economic front in a major drive to revitalize production and meet foreign trade commitments.

---

[47]See "Statement by the Cuban Party and Government on the Imperialist Intervention in Grenada," *Granma Weekly Review*, October 30, 1983, p. 1.

[48]See Castro's speech in *Granma Weekly Review*, December 23, 1984.

Meanwhile, Castro pursued a major public relations offensive in the U.S. media, aimed in part at derailing Radio Martí. Much to his surprise and outrage, however, Radio Martí commenced broadcasting on May 20, shattering his delusions that U.S.-Cuban relations were changing to his benefit. As one sympathetic observer explains:

> Fidel had committed himself to forging a new relationship with the United States. The initial agreement to exchange each country's undesirables was intended to demonstrate that a mutually beneficial relationship was possible.... A month before the Radio Martí confrontation, Castro told me that Ronald Reagan was the one President who could negotiate a rapprochement with Cuba—as Richard M. Nixon did with China—because no one could accuse Reagan of being soft on communism.[49]

Having failed, Castro again reversed his policy toward Washington by immediately canceling not only the migration agreement that he had so tortuously defended only five months earlier, but also the 1979 agreement under which Cuban-Americans could visit relatives on the island. His outburst prevents Cuba from exporting 20,000 of its "undesirables" annually to the United States and deprives the hard-pressed Cuban economy of an estimated $10 million per annum in purchases by visiting Cuban exiles.

At the very least, the more astute leaders within the regime must be perturbed by Castro's behavior. First, he virtually put the Cuban population on a war footing for an entire year, at considerable economic cost, only to abruptly declare war on the malfunctioning economy. Next, he miscalculated in believing that he could influence the Reagan administration's policy with the migration agreement and a media blitz. Finally, by impulsively reacting to Radio Martí, he showed a capacity for irrational decisionmaking under stress at a time when Cuba faces not only a more difficult adversary in the United States, but also difficult political and economic problems on the home front.

Whither Castro?

To overcome his erratic leadership image, Castro must search for new triumphs abroad rather than at home. This may be the intent of his new offensive toward religion and the Catholic Church in Latin America, although he faces potential domestic risks in engaging Catholicism. A similar motivation may be behind his new obsession

---
[49]Peter Winn, "Radio Martí: Rude Rebuff of Overtures by Castro," *Los Angeles Times*, July 19, 1985, Part II, p. 5.

with Latin America's debt and his convening of a series of meetings in Havana over the debt issue in the summer and fall of 1985. Both issues are relatively risk-free for Cuba, and they also enable him to shift tactically to a pragmatic role as a Latin American statesman and defender of Third World interests at a time when regional and international trends do not favor a more activist foreign policy.

Neither religion nor the debt question, however, promises the kinds of major strategic breakthroughs or concrete gains that appeal most to Castro. They are not of the same magnitude as his military interventions in Angola and Ethiopia or his success in helping to establish new Marxist-Leninist regimes in Nicaragua and Grenada. For the moment, therefore, Castro probably feels frustrated, if not trapped, by adverse trends in the international correlation of forces. There are good reasons for him to be cautious. Yet his hubris-nemesis complex and his rebellious, radical, and opportunistic tendencies will probably compel him, sooner or later, to try to resume the offensive against the United States in pursuit of his maximalist ambitions.

VI. CASTRO'S FOREIGN POLICY OPTIONS

Unless he undergoes a fundamental personality change, which seems unlikely, Castro's basic patterns of thinking and acting are set. Depending on how he views Cuba and the world at any particular time, his response takes the form of either revolutionary maximalism (his preferred policy mode for the long term) or tactical pragmatism (his defensive policy mode for the short term). Each mode represents a distinct *fidelista* way of responding to events and taking initiatives on the international stage. Which one Castro selects, of course, is not entirely up to him; it also depends on the domestic and international forces that constrain or facilitate his actions.

TWO POLICY MODES

This section identifies Castro's options for last half of the 1980s and beyond.

A defensive policy of tactical pragmatism. As in the early 1970s, a minimalist course in the late 1980s would see Castro adopting a relatively prudent, defensive foreign policy posture that reflects a concern for his and his nation's security, and a lack of capability or opportunity to do anything truly ambitious. Thus he would seek to preserve established gains, disarm or confuse adversaries, and use rhetoric and diplomatic maneuvers to play upon hot issues. This posture would probably manifest itself in renewed diplomatic overtures toward Latin America, Western Europe, and even the United States, as Castro would seek to project an image of reasonableness as a pragmatic, mature statesman.

Such an apparently prudent course must be understood in the context of Castro's mindset and *modus operandi*: Tactical pragmatism would *not* lead to Cuba's accommodation with the United States, or to curtailment of its close military collaboration with the Soviet Union, or to cessation of its revolutionary subversive activities in the Western Hemisphere, or to the termination of its military interventionism under the guise of "proletarian internationalism." At the very least, Cuba would continue to provide military and security assistance to its clients. Hence, Castro's "pragmatism" should be understood as being "prudent" only in relation to his revolutionary maximalism.

An offensive policy of revolutionary maximalism. As in the post-1975 period, a maximalist course of action would see Castro aggressively pursuing his maximum foreign policy objectives. These include:

- Leading the Third World anti-imperialist struggle to erode the power and presence of the United States.
- Extending Cuba's influence and presence in Africa and Latin America.
- Promoting the rise of radical-left or Marxist-Leninist regimes in Africa and Latin America that will align themselves with Cuba.
- Expanding Cuba's military capabilities as a regional and global actor.
- Gaining leverage over the Soviet Union to broaden Cuba's freedom of action.

The achievement of these goals would largely be predicated on the use of violence, both conventional (military) and unconventional (guerrilla). Violence is, after all, an essential element of Castro's *modus operandi*; it has been present in all his major successes, from the triumph over Batista, through the African operations, to Nicaragua today. The role of violence is what ultimately distinguishes revolutionary maximalism from tactical pragmatism.

Under a maximalist strategy, therefore, Castro would continue to recruit, train, and support revolutionaries for guerrilla activities in their homelands. He would be disposed to increase the Cuban combat presence overseas (Angola, Ethiopia) or perhaps even to dispatch additional combat troops on new "internationalist" missions (Nicaragua, Namibia). He would aggressively seek to exploit new targets of opportunity in the Third World, not only to damage the United States, but also to oblige the Soviet Union to resume the international offensive, thereby enhancing Cuba's value to Moscow in its role as a military as well as political paladin in the Third World.

Which of these policy modes is Castro likely to emphasize? He would surely prefer to embark upon a maximalist course, but he apparently finds that he must presently remain in a pragmatic mode for domestic and international reasons. If these constraints persist, the *líder máximo* could become locked into a policy of relative pragmatism during his waning years—an outcome he would undoubtedly regard as frustrating and perhaps intolerable.

In the meantime, in assessing his future options, Castro is certain to distinguish between a short- to medium-term time frame that will take him through the end of the Reagan administration (January 1989) and a longer-term perspective into the 1990s when a less assertive U.S.

administration may be in office and a stronger, more expansionist Soviet Union may reemerge. Because there is greater certainty and policy relevance in a short- to medium-term analysis, we shall focus on Castro's policy options through the end of the 1980s.

KEY VARIABLES IN CASTRO'S FUTURE POLICY CALCULUS

As he awaits the end of the Reagan administration, Castro is likely to weigh (1) Cuba's domestic situation, (2) the U.S. posture, (3) the Soviet position, (4) the openings in the Third World, and (5) the political and military situation of Cuba's clients, in order to determine which mode he prefers. Of these five factors, the Soviet position may be the most critical for Castro, because Moscow ultimately sets the parameters within which he may operate.[1] Still, as a rule of thumb:

- The more favorable his assessments are with regard to each of these five situation factors, especially on the international front and with respect to the Soviet Union, the more inclined he will be to resume a maximalist revolutionary strategy.
- The less favorable his assessment, the more obliged he will be to opt for tactical pragmatism and await more favorable developments.

Cuba's domestic situation. Although manageable, the current state of the economy, intra-elite balances, and regime-mass relations do not allow Castro much leeway to pursue new adventures abroad. He may be counting on the significant upturn in the world market price of sugar to bolster the economy in 1986–87, but drought, Hurricane Kate, and sugar export commitments to the Soviets will limit the extent to which Cuba could benefit from such an increase. Nor will Cuba's reexport of surplus Soviet oil earn as much revenue as before, at today's lower prices. A new round of economic hardship and radicalism, both signaled by the recent abolition of the peasant free market, will intensify popular discontent and emigration pressures. Still, Cuba will survive economically because the Soviet Union cannot afford to lose its most important Third World client, while political controls and organized mass support will further ensure the regime's survival. In sum, problems at home will not compel Castro to turn inward and relent

---

[1]Castro and Cuba may need to key off the Soviets more than ever, not only because of economic dependence, but also because Third World, Latin American, and other international frameworks are not as available and amenable to Castro's manipulations as they have been in the past.

from his international activism. He may even be able to delegate greater domestic policy authority to Raúl and concentrate on international affairs. He needs new exploits abroad to strengthen his position internally, but he must take care not to further jeopardize his leadership image or the interests of the Cuban armed forces.

The posture of the United States. The Reagan administration has committed itself to rolling back Communist advances in Central America, southern Africa, and elsewhere. Nicaragua may be central to this strategy because it lies within the U.S. sphere of influence, thus making it essential to the strategy's credibility. In the meantime, growing American frustration with international terrorism and low-intensity conflicts have already led to the use of military force against Libya. Castro has surely observed that the administration's tougher anti-Communist and anti-terrorist stance has gained increasing support from Congress and the American people. It has become far more difficult for Castro to manipulate the American political process.

The position of the Soviet Union. Gorbachev is rapidly consolidating his power, appointing new leaders with whom Castro is less familiar. The Soviet regime is also concentrating on economic revitalization at home and insisting that its clients, including Cuba, adopt policy and even leadership changes to improve their own economic performance. Since the November 1985 summit meeting between Reagan and Gorbachev, Moscow has given high priority to stabilizing the Soviet-American relationship. In keeping with its reassessment of Soviet policy in the Third World, this priority may lead Moscow to avoid new commitments and confrontations there—witness the withdrawal of Soviet naval vessels prior to the U.S. airstrikes against Libya. None of this meets Castro's desires for an expansionist Soviet foreign policy predicated on military might. At the same time, however, Moscow is trying to consolidate and preserve its gains in Afghanistan, South Yemen, Ethiopia, Angola, and Nicaragua. For Castro, Soviet commitments to the latter two countries hold out prospects for a continued if not expanded Cuban role as an international paladin. This prospect, along with Soviet-approved changes in Cuba's internal affairs, could lead to improved cooperation with Moscow.

Third World targets of opportunity. The Third World presently offers few visible opportunities for Castro to make military and revolutionary breakthroughs like those of the middle to late 1970s. The conditions that favored Cuba's military interventionism then are not present now: The United States is challenging Communist advances; the Soviet empire is consolidating rather than expanding; Cuban military interventionism cannot be so easily legitimized; and the local military situation poses risks for Cuban troops in Angola and especially in

Nicaragua if Cuba elects to intervene there. This does not mean that no new opportunity will appear; rather, Castro is apparently not optimistic about the current revolutionary potential of the Third World. His major opportunity on the horizon appears to be in southern Africa, where he may aspire to play a leading role in helping liberate South Africa from apartheid rule.

The status of Cuba's client-states. Both Angola and Nicaragua face internal anti-Communist insurgencies supported by external powers. U.S. assistance to the rebels in both countries has increased, posing some threat to the survival of the regimes. However, the Contras in Nicaragua have made little headway, and it may take two or three more years before they become a significant military problem for the regime. Meanwhile, the Soviets are backing Managua by providing military assistance to combat the Contras. In Angola, the economy has been hurt by the sharp reduction in oil revenues, but the Soviets appear committed to ensuring the survival of the MPLA, by military means if necessary. They provided greater levels of assistance to enable the MPLA, backed by Cuban troops and Soviet military advisers, to resume the offensive against UNITA in 1986. However, a further escalation of the Cuban involvement in Angola could tie down Cuban forces, while a worsening of the Nicaraguan situation could result in a U.S. threat to Cuba itself.

Taken together, these five situation factors do not currently favor a strategy of revolutionary maximalism. Castro likes to believe that he can ride if not command some inevitable change in the forces of history. Yet there appears to be little at present to elicit this sense of inevitability. He may decide that the domestic and client-state situations might allow room for heightened Cuban internationalism; however, there are major risks (the U.S. factor), constraints (the Soviet factor), and few opportunities (the Third World factor) for him to try to resume the revolutionary offensive. Since the Grenada debacle of 1983, Castro's foreign policy behavior has thus approximated tactical pragmatism.

ALTERNATIVE SITUATION SCENARIOS AND CASTRO'S OPTIONS

How these situation factors play out over the next three or four years should determine whether Castro will shift to the offensive or maintain a more defensive posture. Accordingly, two alternative scenarios, or future projections, are presented below, each involving a different combination of situation factors. These scenarios are *illustra-*

tive only. They are constructed to show the kinds of plausible situations that could incline Castro to pursue one policy/strategy mode over the other, consistent with his hubris-nemesis complex and radical *modus operandi*.

Unless Castro himself should become seriously ill or die, it does not appear that the next few years are likely to provide significant changes in Cuba's internal situation. Therefore, although Castro might have to cope with serious migration pressures, the domestic situation is held constant, as described above, in both of the following scenarios.[2]

Risks and Constraints: Tactical Pragmatism

If the present status of international factors persists—continuing danger from the United States, a still cautious Soviet Union, few Third World openings, and insurgent opposition to the Angolan and Nicaraguan regimes—Castro will probably continue to opt for a prudent course over the short to medium term, biding his time and awaiting more favorable developments in the positions of the two superpowers and in the Third World.

He is likely to continue pursuing his global ambitions at a lower level of confrontation, but still with a high level of rhetorical visibility and demagoguery. This has already occurred concerning the Latin American debt crisis and may be developed further with religious issues.[3] By insinuating himself into the camp of liberation theology, he may aspire to divide the Catholic Church, lay the groundwork for a "united front" of Marxist and Catholic revolutionaries, and shield Nicaragua and Cuba from the United States.

Yet Castro is not so constrained and frustrated—as he was in the early 1970s—that he is likely to temporarily forgo unconventional, revolutionary warfare. He will surely continue Cuba's support of guerrilla violence in El Salvador, although the present situation is not encouraging for the FMLN. And he may be tempted to stir up trouble in other countries in the region.[4] At the very least, the threat of

---

[2]Under either scenario, Castro might respond to mounting migration pressures by deliberately creating a new, Mariel-like exodus that, in addition to easing internal discontent, would put the Reagan administration on the defensive. Castro would have to take care, however, not to provoke the United States by his action.

[3]Castro's radical stances, as in the debt issue, expand Latin American perceptions of their bargaining latitude vis-a-vis the United States. Castro shifts the spectrum to the left, but this does not really result in leadership for him, and it is not clear that this role is gratifying to him.

[4]Besides Chile, the opportunities may include Panama, where the Soviet Union and Cuba have extensive ties; Puerto Rico, where Cuba has supported separatist revolutionaries; Haiti, where Duvalier's successors face enormous social, economic, and political problems; the Dominican Republic, where economic and political stability remains frag-

Cuban-backed subversion may be used as a tactic of political extortion against selected governments, especially in Latin America, or as a potential bargaining tool in his game against the United States. Castro may continue to hope that Cuban support for revolutionary subversion will ultimately lead to the installation of a new radical regime somewhere, as occurred in Grenada and Nicaragua in 1979. But in consonance with a strategy of tactical pragmatism, he will aim primarily at advancing Cuba's interests in state-to-state relations.

Castro will be careful to operate at less visible levels to diminish the possibility of U.S. retaliation. He knows that he must not become closely identified with terrorists in Central America and the Caribbean, if only because of the growing American consensus against terrorism. Hence, he will continue his efforts to disassociate Cuba from Libyan activities in the region. While Castro's views about terrorism remain obscure, he apparently has objections to its offensive use in creating Marxist-Leninist revolutions, although he may not be averse to its use to defend a state or people from attack by a stronger power.

However Castro decides to mix violence and statesmanship in his version of tactical pragmatism, he will do everything he can not to abandon his Third World clients as long as he can avoid a direct military confrontation with the United States. He has already suffered criticism from leftist quarters for not rendering greater support to the Coard regime at the time of the invasion of Grenada. And he has an enormous strategic stake in preserving his new allies in Angola and Nicaragua.

He will probably continue sending military and security advisers to Nicaragua to help the regime consolidate its power. He will also assist the Sandinista army in its struggle against the Contras by continuing to send Cuban advisers down to the battalion level and by supplying Cuban helicopter pilots and other skilled personnel to help operate Soviet heavy weapons.

He will remain adamant in rejecting an arrangement that would link Namibia's independence with the withdrawal of Cuban combat forces from Angola. In his view, their presence is required to ensure the consolidation of the MPLA regime.[5] If assured of direct Soviet support, he

---

ile; and possibly Mexico, where Castro may want to use leftist elements to remind the de la Madrid administration and its successor of Havana's potential for making mischief and becoming a player if a violent upheaval were ever to occur in that country.

[5]Castro reaffirmed this position in his report to the Third Party Congress: "The old attempt to link Namibia's independence with the withdrawal of the Cuban internationalist contingent has faced a decisive rejection from the international community. . . . The independence of Namibia, an end to aggression against Angola, and an end to aid to UNITA . . . would make feasible the gradual withdrawal of part of those forces, as Angola and Cuba have proposed. However, whether the remaining forces continue in

may even be inclined to increase their presence to help the MPLA defeat the UNITA insurgency. In fact, Castro has already indicated a readiness to step up Cuba's commitment to Angola: On May 29, 1985, he warned that he was prepared to send another 200,000 Cubans to Angola in the years ahead to match those who had already served in Africa.[6] He may believe that such a move might not carry a high risk of U.S. military retaliation against Cuba, although Cuban combat forces might find themselves fighting the South Africans. Still, an escalated Cuban role could have a veneer of legitimacy if Cuban reinforcements were requested by the MPLA government, particularly if South African "aggression" against Angola was at issue.

In both the Nicaraguan and Angolan situations, however, tactical pragmatism would incline Castro toward maintaining a low profile to minimize his military and political risks. He would seek to limit the magnitude of direct Cuban involvement in combat operations, for example, by limiting Cuban forces to air and ground support of MPLA troops.

Whatever the specifics of his support for Angola and Nicaragua, Castro will try to defuse international reaction by appearing to be potentially conciliatory and reasonable. That is essential to his guise of tactical pragmatism. For Latin American, West European, and U.S. audiences, he will probably continue voicing support for the Contadora process, the repudiation of military solutions to the Central American crisis, and the withdrawal of foreign military forces from the region. To further deflect U.S. policy and divide the U.S. public, he might indicate, through the U.S. media or other unofficial channels, his readiness to make concessions on *marginal* issues affecting U.S.-Cuban relations, such as migration, hijacking, or even drug enforcement. On Angola, he might continue proposing a phased withdrawal of Cuban forces, but only if Namibia became independent, aid to UNITA were cut, and the MPLA regime were secure.

New Opportunities and Risks: Revolutionary Maximalism

In contrast to the first scenario, a different set of developments could incline Castro to resume the offensive as a revolutionary maxi-

---

Angola and the circumstances and the date when all of them should be withdrawn, is the exclusive prerogative of the peoples of Angola and Cuba." (From *FBIS*, February 7, 1986, p. Q57.)

[6]Asserting that Cubans always fulfilled their "internationalist duty," he added, "And if more soldiers are needed, we will send more soldiers because in the face of every attack by imperialism and racism, we have always reacted by reinforcing Angola and there are still a number of Cubans there, always prepared, alert and ready to fight in the face of any enemy escalation. We have always been Angola's reinforcements." (*Granma Weekly Review*, June 9, 1985, p. 3.)

malist. In this case, we assume that Cuba's domestic situation and the U.S. posture remain essentially the same as above. However, major changes have occurred regarding the Soviet posture, Third World targets of opportunity, and the status of Cuba's two clients.

The Soviet Union. Gorbachev has consolidated his leadership, the Soviet domestic situation is under control, and both Party and military circles believe that the international correlation of forces is again shifting in favor of the socialist bloc and "progressive" forces.[7] The Soviet Union is again inclined to flex its muscles as a global power.

South Africa. The South African situation deteriorates, and there is organized guerrilla violence by the African National Congress (ANC). The ANC is actively supported by Angola, Zambia, Zimbabwe, and Tanzania. Because of its domestic and foreign actions (possibly including military strikes against the first three states above), Pretoria finds itself increasingly isolated internationally as a result of West European, Third World, and U.S. condemnation of its policies.

Angola. The military situation shifts in favor of the MPLA. Backed and trained by Cuban and Soviet military personnel, the combat proficiency of the MPLA forces steadily improves in the fight against the UNITA forces led by Savimbi. Preoccupied with its own internal turmoil, South Africa lessens its military backing of the UNITA forces. Covert U.S. support for Savimbi is insufficient to make up the difference. Seeking to exploit the situation, the Soviets step up their assistance to the MPLA to assure the latter's victory over UNITA, while also increasing their aid to SWAPO (the South-West African People's Organization) in Namibia.

Nicaragua. The military situation turns advantageous to the FSLN regime as a result of Soviet and Cuban military assistance and the improved combat proficiency of the Sandinista army. The Contras find themselves overmatched despite U.S. private and public assistance and are unable to hold ground in Nicaragua. Meanwhile, the Honduran government shows signs of wanting to cut its own deal with Managua in return for expelling the Contras from Honduras. Faced with these adverse trends, including a growing Cuban-Soviet foothold in Central America, Washington is seriously considering direct U.S. military action against the Marxist-Leninist regime in Nicaragua.

Overall, this projection holds out the prospect of a major loss for Castro, but also opportunities for major breakthroughs—possibly the use of Cuba's military (and subversive) forces to support Angola or Nicaragua for a grand "internationalist" cause. However, Castro

---

[7]For example, the Soviets might perceive a more favorable international correlation of forces because of turmoil in South Africa, the Philippines, or a pro-Western state in the Middle East.

cannot expect the United States to stand idly by. His options may thus also involve enormous risks to Cuba's security and his own power. How might Castro respond if he opts for revolutionary maximalism?

Responding to Nicaragua. The consolidation of the Sandinista regime would represent a major setback for the United States, and it would ensure Cuba's power and presence on the American mainland. But if the prospect of such a consolidation grows near, the danger of a U.S. military assault to dislodge the regime may grow proportionally. Worse yet, if Castro then refrains from sending Cuban troops into Nicaragua, the United States might still elect to neutralize Cuba's own military installations to assure the success of the U.S. assault on Nicaragua.

At the very least, Castro would work hard to head off potential U.S. aggression against Nicaragua or Cuba by maneuvering on the diplomatic and political fronts. He surely would try to enlist the principal Latin American players—including Mexico, Colombia, and Venezuela—in a major diplomatic offensive to stem U.S. military moves, either through the use of Contadora or some other coalition vehicle. He would appeal to West European countries, and possibly the United Nations. He probably would mount a major public relations campaign within the United States in an effort to restrain the administration, and he might advise Managua to adopt a conciliatory posture regarding both Nicaragua's domestic political situation and Central American security. He might propose a security settlement for the region that would combine a Cuban withdrawal from Nicaragua, international support for a "benign" Sandinista regime, and the "demilitarization" of the region, with a requirement of U.S. non-aggression guarantees.

If nothing served to constrain the United States, would Castro dispatch Cuban combat troops to Nicaragua? Following the U.S.-East Caribbean action in Grenada, he acknowledged that Cuba's limited capabilities would prevent it from defending Nicaragua, a position that was reconfirmed by Vice President Carlos Rafael Rodríguez during his May 1986 trip to South America.[8] Thus, a prospective U.S. intervention in Nicaragua would present him with a serious dilemma: He would risk losing an important ally in Central America if he did not defend Nicaragua, but he might risk a military showdown with the United States if he did.

To gain a protective cloak of legitimacy and thereby minimize the possibility of U.S. retaliation, Castro might try to aid Nicaragua

---

[8]In a televised interview in Buenos Aires, Rodríguez stated that Cuba is "not in a position to break a U.S. air and naval blockade against Nicaragua because Cuba's forces are defensive." (*FBIS*, June 3, 1986, p. B3.)

directly by enlisting international participation, particularly from Latin America. In that event, he could conceivably send Cuban "volunteers" as a part of a larger "internationalist" military force that Cuba would help organize and ferry to Nicaragua. But such a gambit also would present problems for him. It would pose major organizational and logistical difficulties for Cuba, and it might well be vetoed by Moscow for fear that Cuba's involvement in a multilateral action could still precipitate a U.S. attack on Cuba itself.

Finally, Castro might also encounter strong resistance from the FAR if his military involvement in Nicaragua were seen as potentially suicidal—as was the case with his no-surrender order to Cuban forces on Grenada. On balance, therefore, it would seem that Castro would not respond to imminent U.S. aggression in Nicaragua by dispatching Cuban combat forces there.[9]

Responding in southern Africa. To escape his dilemma, Castro may prefer to resume the revolutionary offensive in southern Africa and, by so doing, link Nicaragua's security with a Cuban escalation in Angola and possibly Namibia as well. He might well calculate that he can count on needed Soviet support for a Cuban escalation because of Moscow's strong commitment to Angola, greater interest in further extending its influence in southern Africa, and the lower risk of a direct confrontation with the United States.

Specifically, through an increased Cuban conventional military and subversive role in southern Africa, Castro might aspire to:

- Destroy UNITA and assure the permanency of the MPLA in Angola.
- Intensify the guerrilla struggle by SWAPO in Namibia.
- Mobilize international support for war against South Africa.
- Put imperialism on the defensive in southern Africa.
- Reclaim Third World leadership and a measure of leverage over Moscow.

Castro may also aspire to constrain U.S. policy toward Nicaragua if Washington perceives that its larger interests are in jeopardy in South Africa.

---

[9]Still, such an option cannot be entirely ruled out, given Castro's mindset. Were he to feel that the Nicaraguan situation was hopeless, that the Soviets were about to abandon him and his Nicaraguan ally, that the United States was on the verge of winning, and that Latin Americans would generally applaud him, he might feel tempted to overcome FAR and Soviet opposition—and thus assure his place in history by one grand gesture of ultimate defiance against imperialism.

How might Castro pursue such a maximalist strategy? Having secured Soviet permission and support, he could increase Cuba's military presence on behalf of the MPLA, with Cuban forces assuming a direct combat role in Angola, for example, by flying ground support missions against UNITA, providing air cover for MPLA troops, and perhaps even spearheading a new offensive as the Cuban expeditionary force did in the Ogaden in 1977–78.[10] An intensified Cuban role in Angola could be expanded into Namibia and perhaps even into troubled South Africa as well by actively backing SWAPO and the ANC, respectively. Castro could justify such a policy as a national war of liberation against South Africa's hated apartheid regime. In so doing, he could rally Black Africa's support and, at the same time, help legitimize the Soviet foothold in southern Africa.

Such a gambit would be tantamount to a *fidelista* version of lateral escalation, whereby Castro would seek to intensify crisis conditions in southern Africa to distract and constrain the United States from intervening in Nicaragua. Indeed, his past calls for the creation of "new Sierra Maestras" and "many Vietnams" indicate that, as a global strategist, he has long thought about how to divide U.S. attention and military capabilities in just such a fashion. Were he to succeed, he would triumph anew on both the African and Central American fronts.

The military and political risks would be high, however. The nearby African states could react negatively and condemn the Cuban involvement in southern Africa, particularly if it were seen as simply serving Soviet global ambitions. A protracted, bloody war in Angola involving UNITA and particularly South African forces could lead to heavy Cuban troop casualties and possibly the defeat of the FAR; this could boomerang inside Cuba, causing increased popular unrest or even an officer rebellion.

Nonetheless, this volatile mix of potentially high gains and high risks is consistent with Castro's mindset and past behavior, and a policy may already be in the making. Havana has reportedly approached Moscow to obtain "Soviet clearance and support to issue a formal declaration of war against South Africa to try to turn the struggle against the white regime into an international crusade such as that fought against Hitler."[11] Of course, the report may have been fabri-

---

[10]Since the creation of the 1.5-million-strong MTT, Castro has boasted that Cuba could dispatch 100,000 soldiers to Angola without weakening Cuban defenses. (See *Granma Weekly Review*, June 9, 1985, p. 3.)

[11]This report was based on information given by "a senior government official in Havana" to *The Observer* (London). Among other arguments cited, the official claimed that the Cubans had pressed the Soviets to support a full-scale war on grounds that it would "lift Cuban and Soviet prestige in the Third World and with anti-apartheid campaigners," and that "with enough hardware, they (the Cubans) could win a war against South Africa." (*The Observer*, November 24, 1985.)

cated by the Castro regime as a warning to the United States of Cuba's potential for further destabilizing the South African situation.

Moscow probably would be reluctant to support a Cuban initiative to wage full-scale war against South Africa. But Castro need not propose such an ambitious Cuban-led offensive. He could present it in the form of a Cuban military buildup in Angola that, if it won the war there, might open opportunities for further expansion into Namibia. The Soviets would be more likely to be receptive to that type of proposal than to the dispatch of Cuban troops to Nicaragua.

Castro may thus decide to adopt a maximalist revolutionary posture toward Angola and South Africa if he feels confident that:

- Cuba can count on Soviet backing to wage an all-out offensive in Angola and increase assistance to SWAPO guerrilla forces in Namibia. (This would strengthen Cuba's value to and leverage over Moscow.)
- Were South Africa to retaliate in Angola or Namibia, Havana could call for a full-scale war by African states against Pretoria in which Cuban contingents could participate in large-scale or commando-type operations.
- By forcing events in this way, Castro would oblige Moscow to resume the kind of expansionist drive into southern Africa that characterized Soviet policy beginning in the mid-1970s.
- Because of international condemnation of South Africa's apartheid regime and U.S. absorption in attending to security issues there, the United States would be constrained from attacking Cuba.
- Preoccupied with the unraveling of the political and military situation in southern Africa, the United States might also be restrained from attacking Nicaragua.

Castro would, of course, have to face many practical problems and risks—among them, logistical difficulties in southern Africa, likely clashes with superior South African forces, overextension of Cuba's military commitments, increased vulnerability to U.S. counterescalation in Nicaragua, and likely resistance from the Cuban military. Yet, his capacity to think globally and act as a player on the world stage should not be underestimated as it was in the 1970s. Nor should it be forgotten that his hubris-nemesis complex and audacious *modus operandi* could lead him to try to deal the United States a strategic defeat through renewed Cuban military (or guerrilla) involvement in the Third World, particularly southern Africa.